Confessions of a Potty-Mouthed Chef: How to Cheat, Eat and Be Happy!

(one woman's quest for fulfillment
in the kitchen and the bedroom)

Vickie van Dyke

Tellwell Talent
www.tellwell.ca

ISBN
978-0-2288-2882-2 (Hardcover)
978-0-2288-2880-8 (Paperback)
978-0-2288-2881-5 (eBook)

For the guy who taught me the true meaning of
"love of my life" — my son, Sam.

Don't judge me by my past. I don't live there anymore.
(Oscar Auliq-Ice)

The names in this memoir have been changed to protect the
innocent. Shiloh (my dog) and I remain guilty as charged.
- Vickie

Foreword

I've known Vickie for many years through a beautiful friendship, shared musical passions, our mutual love of the written word and oh yes: wine — lots and lots of wine. I fell in love with this memoir when I read the first incarnation ten years ago. Much like life itself, the book has evolved and found its true voice — you're in for quite the ride. Vickie's adventure reads much like her secret diary opened for all to see.

Her wild and crazy journey through the halls of mating, marrying, parenting, dating, cheating and cooking is such an honest recounting of an unanticipated life, you will most certainly find yourself laughing, crying and yes, cheating. Much like Murphy's Law, Vickie learns that life can turn itself upside down in the same time it takes to boil a three-minute egg. And even when that egg lands on your face, you soldier on.

If you looked up "honest" and "raw" in the dictionary you'd find **Vickie van Dyke** in bold letters. Call it insanity or bravado, Vickie paints a beautiful, sometimes raunchy and sometimes painful picture of life's foibles in her search for her true heart song. She learns that if the dream doesn't come true, change the dream. Bravo my friend!

When it comes to those cheating recipes, there is no one I know more out of the box (can, jar, package) than the witty, saucy and sometimes sarcastic Ms. van Dyke. This is definitely not your mama's cookbook. So hold on to your hat and get ready to take a closer look in your pantry! We should all have this much fun in and out of the kitchen!

Jacqui Brown — author of *Bitch Please!*, *The Art of Giving a Fuck* and *The Mojo Manual*

Table of Contents

Prologue

"BUT I DON'T WANNA GO."

I'm whining. I know I am. I'm whining with a bit of snivel thrown in. I am lying on the sofa with a pillow on my belly and I am pouting like a petulant teenager.

"We're going, Vickie," responds my darling husband as he downs the last of his beer. "Stop acting like a petulant teenager."

I hate when he does that. You know. Calls me on my shit.

It's the day after Boxing Day. You know, the day after the day after Christmas. I am ready for bed. I'm exhausted to the brink of falling flat on my puffy, over-made-up, over-celebrated, over-drunken face. I am completely done with chestnuts-a-roasting, bells-a-jingling and balsam needles-a-vacuuming. The holiday season (which I dearly love) has had its way with me. Endless dinner parties, cocktail parties, office parties and family parties, many of which I have facilitated personally, have done me in but good.

I've just come home from working my day job. I say *day* job because for me it really is just a *day* job — I only work one day a week. Sounds like a joyride but trust me, my one day is a mental marathon (more on that later) and the hour-long winter commute hasn't helped. Especially so as it falls hard on the heels of all that joyous jubilation. December 27 can bite me. I need a nap!

"C'mon honey, get your coat and let's just go." He lovingly tousles my uncombed hair. "We promised."

We promised. Sure we did. We promised three weeks before every damn hall got decked and then redecked and then decked again. All I want now is a silent night. Maybe a bit of leftover turkey, a long soak in the hot tub and my big old bed.

But only in my dreams. Because turns out no one shared this plan with our next door neighbours. And they have invited us for dinner. Fab. Frigging fab. More merriment. More food, more fake smiles, more fa-la-la and more keeping my eyes open. I can hardly wait.

"Honey baby sweetie," I snivel louder, "couldn't we just feign illness, accident or maybe even death?" I know. Can you spell drama queen? "Pretty please can we cancel?"

Honey baby sweetie is unusually resolute. And just so you know, I call him honey baby sweetie because he calls me honey baby sweetie. Or HBS. I'm not entirely sure how this happened. We just couldn't settle on one term of endearment so we amalgamated a bunch. Also, we think we're pretty damn funny. One thing HBS and I have in common is sense of humour.

"No," HBS commands gently. "We're going. We promised. They've been here a dozen times and we've never ever dined at their house. They invited. You said yes. Now get off that couch and put your party face on."

Yeah sure, blame it on me. But he is not wrong. Apart from today, I typically crave distraction.

"We won't stay late. We will eat, drink and run. Two hours tops. I promise."

I close my eyes and briefly mull this offer. I know I should redo my make-up, change into a flirty little number, put my hair up into a sexy ponytail and spritz on the Chanel. But I just can't seem to locate my give-a-shit chip. So I drag my weary ass off the sofa, powder my nose, run a brush through my hair and that is the end of my *toilette.*

We bundle up because Ontario winter is raging and stumble down our country road, dragging our very reluctant nine-year-old son behind us. See, Jack really doesn't want to go either. He has new toys demanding his attention. New movies to watch. Old people are boring. The neighbours have no kids his age. But it doesn't matter. My normally easy-going hubby has laid down the law and insisted. To both of us.

In hindsight, the irony here is staggering. Little does HBS know he is about to expedite the unravelling of his seemingly perfect family. The implosion has begun. On a sleepy night when the world should be at peace ours is about to be shattered. Forever. Perfect family be damned.

Perfect family. It's what we are. Or at least what we appear to be. The living embodiment of a Pepsi commercial. Successful, attractive and loving with a vast circle of equally fabulous friends. Cottages, sailboats, swimming pools and world travel. Gold, diamonds, clothes and cars. HBS has a successful business, I have a successful one-day job. We have a darling boy who attends private school. We have a dog and a cat. We live on seventy-nine acres in a house we designed and had custom built (with clever hubby doing much of the work himself!). It has soaring ceilings, a three-sided fireplace and a hot tub, damnit! I am certainly lacking nothing. Nothing tangible, that is.

Which is why it always bewilders me when I find myself weeping on the kitchen floor during playtime for the boys just prior to dinner *en famile*. There is wine, there is music (usually something jazz-ish), there is candlelight and there are tears. Lots and lots of muffled tears as my boys, none the wiser, frolic on the lower level.

My husband knows nothing of my pain. I have tried to share with him on a few occasions, but he doesn't much like confrontation and his *veddy* British upbringing advocates a more "sweep under the rug" approach. Truth be told I don't really understand my pain either. I just know I am far too frequently empty. Too empty to be filled up by my marriage, my job, my friends or even motherhood. I am an expert at putting on a show (what with my drama degree and all). I just can't figure out real and honest contentment.

It is unlikely tonight's festivities will change any of that. But it is showtime!

The neighbour's home is delightfully warm, inviting and filled with yummy cooking smells. Suddenly I am ravenous.

"Hey guys, you made it!" our host greets us enthusiastically. "Come on in and let's get you a drink!"

No festive fatigue here. Yay him. He takes our coats and leads us into the newly-renovated kitchen where his wife is stirring something savory on the stove. It's all looking pretty good, think I. New appliances, new floor, new cupboards, all very chic. Even a brand new farmhouse table. At which sits a strange couple. Not strange in that they look weird or have green skin or anything, but strange in that we don't know them.

Except we *sort of* do. I look at her smiling face and immediately blurt, "Oh my God, it's you!"

She laughs with great gusto and replies, "Yes, we finally meet!"

We have spoken on the phone many times, she and I, ever since these same mutual neighbours (we live out in the country so "neighbour" is a relative term) recommended her younger daughter as a potential babysitter. We have joked around, compared parenting notes and even discussed a possible ski day together. She is very much like me, this new neighbour/friend. Outgoing, a little brassy, and I'm thinking possibly more fun than monkeys in a barrel. I like fun and I like fun friends and we've never actually met in person before and now here she is. How cool! I am starting to wake up.

Then I look at the man sitting next to her. He is grinning at me with a smile that starts in his belly, detours through his heart and then bursts out through his lips like an exploding firecracker. The faded burn-like scar on his cheek saves his adoringly boyish good looks from absurdity. He is so damn cute I can't speak. And his obvious delight in making my acquaintance is palpable. He reaches across the table to shake my hand and the touch of his skin sends tiny rockets into my bloodstream.

"Hi Vickie," he coos, the smile now almost swallowing his face. "I have heard so much about you, and it is so good to finally meet you."

I forget my fatigue, my hunger, my neighbours, my child, my husband and most likely my own name. I am suddenly wide awake. Strangely speechless. And absolutely terrified to the tips of my toes. Because as I absorb his smile, his scar, his laughing eyes and his velvet fingers I realize with complete certainty that I have just met the love of my life.

Fuck.

Introduction

THE FIRST THING YOU SHOULD KNOW ABOUT ME IS I AM A CHEATER. A very proud cheater too. I've been cheating for a long time. I don't have a problem with it and neither do my friends. I know a lot of people who have never cheated and never will. They stand on their high and mighty pedestals spouting all kinds of platitudes about honour, integrity and truth.

Whatever.

For me, it's all about the end result. And if cheating will get me there faster, easier and without guilt, why wouldn't I?

Yes, my name is Vickie van Dyke and I am a cheater.

We're talking cooking here. Creating culinary delights. Enjoying time in the kitchen. I mean, I will admit to a few adventuresome missteps in other areas of my life — cheating missteps that were not and never will be a source of pride — and we'll get to those soon enough. But for now, it's all about cooking!

Well, maybe not *all*. Just ask any of my former boyfriends. I am known to digress and I'm sure I will since I already am. But the point of this book, besides saving you from a wealth of my own personally tested errors both in and out of the kitchen, is quite simple: how do you learn to love to cook? The easy way. No intimidation, no vexation, no frustration — just good plain ole cookin' cheatin' fun!

Yep, I'm not one of those chi-chi chefs who prides herself on concocting every morsel from the ground up. *Dahling, of course I made this lobster bisque this morning just after I emptied my traps, milked the cows for fresh cream and pulled organic chives from my garden.*

Hell no! I willingly — almost gleefully — open cans of soup, even no-name brands! I buy ready-made sauces, use muffin mixes and boxed potatoes, and I promise I will never, never, ever make a pizza crust from scratch. I truly mean that! Never, ever. The only thing that's ever going to get rolled on my kitchen counter is me, thank you very much. I would rather hit myself over the head with a rolling pin than flatten out pizza dough.

I feel the same way about traditional pie crusts. Wait till you try my easy-as-pie (pun intended) shortbread crust — no rolling required! Honestly, the only time I ever had any fun with a crust of any kind was right after my husband and I split up and I didn't have a rolling pin. I was determined to master pizza from scratch because his new girlfriend makes dandies and I am only just a tiny little bit maybe hugely competitive. So, in the absence of the proper rolling device, I used a wine bottle. It was full when I started and empty when I finished. There was flour and gooey bits of dough and splashes of wine all over the kitchen. I mean, really, have you ever tried rolling dough with an open bottle of wine? However, I was happy (and tipsy) because I surrendered.

Some things in life you simply must accept and surrender to. Wrinkles and gray hair? Middle-aged spread? The end of a bad marriage? An innate inability to make crust (or even care about said crappy homemade crust)? Surrender.

Several glasses of a nice Sauvignon Blanc will help with this.

As I removed dough from my hair, ceiling and wine glass, I decided I was done forever with homemade pizza crusts. And pie crusts be damned as well! Why bother when there are so many wonderful and tasty ready-to-top flatbreads available at your friendly neighbourhood store? I would much rather save my creativity for what goes *on* the pizza, not what goes (at least in my world) into the garbage.

My favourite cooking expression is not and never shall be "from scratch." I used to have a girlfriend — and I say *used to* because she is that very same uber-cook now living with my ex-husband — who prides herself on making everything "from scratch." Baking, cooking, it matters not. All built from the ground up. She is damn good at it. Highly organic. I mean, I don't think they've invested in cows or a wheat field but she plants her own garden and everything. She fertilizes with manure. Real cow poop. She even hangs old loaves of bread to dry out and then somehow they magically become breadcrumbs. I am not kidding.

Not this girl My favourite cooking expressions are "easy-peasy-lemon-squeezy" (borrowed from my son) and "homemade." Because there is a big difference between "from scratch" and "homemade." That difference is way less work! And there is absolutely no reason why homemade can't be "easy-peasy-lemon-squeezy."

See, here's the thing: if you make it at home then it is "homemade." Period. End of discussion. Just because you use canned cream of mushroom soup, pasta from a bag and garlic from a jar doesn't in any way diminish the fact that it is homemade. Be proud!

And yes, the whole garlic thing opens another can of worms (preferably gummy). I know you're supposed to buy fresh garlic in those long Gothic strips and store it in a dark place or hang it around your neck to ward off vampires or smarmy ex-boyfriends and then peel, crush, chop, dice or squish it or whatever. I've done all those things. For some reason, garlic is the one thing that this chopaholic (more on that coming up) does not like chopping. Period. So, when I discovered crushed garlic in a jar I just about peed my pants. No muss, no fuss. I also discovered pre-peeled whole garlic cloves, which at least eliminates that first icky peeling step.

That's not to say that you shouldn't or can't use fresh herbs. Of course they are the best. I'm even going to go on record here to say I have been known to have pots of basil and rosemary growing in my kitchen (before they perish because I inevitably forget to water them). I'm just saying don't beat yourself up if you don't feel like doing it the hard way. Frozen or dried stuff can also do the trick.

My friend, Shayann, tells just about everybody we meet that my house is the best restaurant in town. I love that. I love that she loves the food that I prepare, but I also love that she likes to be here. She loves to sit at my kitchen counter, candles always flickering, and watch me create while we sip wine, listen to music and chat. She calls it the "bitchin' kitchen!" We don't always bitch. Sometimes we laugh, sometimes we cry, sometimes we sneak in a few yoga poses (we try to do this before wine) and sometimes we fantasize about our perfect futures.

It's all about the vibe. When I make food there is no stress. I've seen cooks tackle eggs on toast with the same anxiety I would reserve for a root canal or tax audit. Not this gal. I'm not trying to prove anything and I'm not trying to outdo anyone, so I really do love every moment in the kitchen. Please don't hate me but I don't even mind cleaning up. (Word of advice: always do it as you go.) What happens is that love then permeates every action I take. Seriously. I know I'm sounding all new-age philosophical, but it's true. Love permeates every action I take because I have learned to love to cook. Being in love can fuel this process too. One of my favourite singer-songwriters, Melody Gardot, once tweeted "A woman in love is capable of making the most incredible cuisine. She pours into the dish her most passionate senses where others use salt." Beautiful.

However, as you are about to learn, I'm not always in love and then there are those times that I am in love but not loved back and then there are those times when I'm not in love but I am in lust and that conjures up a whole new set of spices. The point is, I am always in love with eating and therefore always in love with cooking.

It wasn't always this way. The eating part, yes. I enjoyed being in the kitchen puttering away. But I didn't truly learn to cook until my husband and I split up many years ago. At that time, I discovered the freedom to cook whatever I wanted in any way I wanted. I discovered new tastes, combinations, spices — and new joy — in the kitchen. There were even a few joyful romps on the counter.

I also discovered that cooking is therapy. And much cheaper than a psychiatrist.

So, if you dare to read on, you will learn exactly why I was in such desperate need of therapy. My life wasn't exactly Betty Crocker aprons and pearls. It wasn't even dime-store cookie cutter romance. It was one big fat constant churning source of frustration, guilt and angst. Much like those damn crusts I will never make.

While we're on the subject of *never* — even though my favourite expression is "never say never and never say forever" — I will never ever own an electric vegetable chopper. Heck, I don't even have an electric can opener and you already know how fond I am of cans. I will also never own a food processor or a bread machine. For crumb's sake — literally — just go to the bakery! That said, I wouldn't mind one of those stand-up-by-themselves mixers. Might be fun to walk away while my no-name cake mix is churning. But I don't even mind my archaic hand-held beater. I mean, it's not that archaic. I remember my mother beating the batter while cranking by hand. I actually feel quite contemporary. For me, the best part of food prep is all the chopping, peeling, mixing, stirring, tasting — whatever it takes to get me where I want to go. Sometimes I don't even have a clue where I want to go until I get there. But I love the journey. The therapeutic journey.

I love the journey so much it even gets a little, um, personal. Because, of course, the cooking journey starts at the grocery store and I'm gonna tell you right here, right now, that supermarkets turn me on. Yes. *That* kind of turn-on. I love shopping for food. I love manhandling fruit, smelling veggies, squeezing fresh bread and drooling over new cans of soup. I love standing in the frozen food aisle freezing my boobies and I even love standing in the check-out line reading tabloid trash. Although I will admit I've recently become a fan of those self-checkouts. Why? Because I get to manhandle, smell and squeeze one more time. It is all big fat sexy fun. Even more fun if I'm doing it with my man.

Anyway, my point is that cooking is fun! It's not stress, it's not pressure and it's not a competition. It's FUN! It doesn't have to be complicated and it doesn't have to be time-consuming. Because at the end of the day, you want to relax and create something that your friends and family will enjoy and SO WILL YOU. After all, you're not just the chef. You get to eat what you make. What better payoff is there?

As for the cheating end of things, let's just say it was cheating that ended my marriage. And yes, let's also admit that I was the one who cheated. Like I said, not exactly my shiniest hour. Yet still an experience from which I learned more life lessons than I ever could have imagined. The cheating led to a whole new life for me. My husband found a whole new love. It inspired a different whole new life for my lover and fellow cheater. And yes, his wife too discovered a whole new life and love.

Okay, it's complicated. But cooking doesn't have to be. So let's get to it. Because my hope is that once you get through this book you won't need it anymore. You'll pay it forward to some other hapless chef and get to creating your own masterpieces, your own fiascos (trust me, I've had many) and your own fun. Then I'll buy your cookbook!

Dating Daze (Don't Be an Artichicken!)

MUCH LIKE SOME MEN, SOME SEXUAL PROCLIVITIES AND SOME BUCKET LIST ITEMS, WE COME TO SOME FOODS LATER IN LIFE. I didn't even know what a mango was till I was about forty. That's about the same time I discovered artichokes. Before that, the very word "artichoke" baffled me, much like rutabaga, okra and turnip. Okay, I know what a turnip is. I just don't like them. But artichokes? No clue.

That was then and this is now and I have recently launched a full-fledged love affair with artichokes. I have no idea how this happened. Was it a moonlit night? Michael Bublé crooning on the stereo? A romantic fire crackling nearby?

Who cares? I'm madly in love with artichokes. And I can assure you this is no passing fling.

Now if you're one of those culinary cowards who cruises by the artichoke section without a second glance, I respectfully urge you to at least give one a try. If not, I'll be forced to label you an *artichicken*. Just like Todd. Let's take a little stroll down memory lane, shall we?

I meet Todd online. Yes, post-marriage and post-lover I begin doing that online dating thing. Believe it or not, this also helps me to become a better chef (stay tuned). Todd is not my first rodeo, nor will he be my last, but following many one-date failures (my girlfriends call me the "one-date wonder" because I never meet anyone who inspires a second meeting) I am a bit of a pro at the process. I can read a looney a mile off and I have learned that lots of emails, texts and phone calls give you a pretty clear picture of the guy. So, when Todd offers to cook me dinner, as opposed to splitting the cheque at a restaurant (standard meet-and-greet procedure), I agree. Nice touch, think I, since I am usually the one at the stove. Also nice since I will be driving two hours to meet the man. But at least it is two hours to the beach. Todd lives in the lakeside town of Southampton (on Lake Huron), purported to have the second best (only to Maui) sunsets in the world. So at least I reckon I'll get a great view even if it doesn't end up being Todd.

It's a beautiful summer day in paradise. I arrive early afternoon (as per Todd's instructions) and find the key to his ramshackle house under the shoe on the front porch (also as instructed). Todd's domicile is a work in progress but it does boast a few nice features like a huge kitchen island (my favourite!) and an open concept main floor complete with double bed (how convenient) at one end. Todd is at work so I am free to explore to my heart's content.

After a brief bit of recon I drive the few blocks into town. The sand beach is long and gorgeous. I take a quick stroll, dip my toes in the warm water and then head to the main street to find the amazing clothing shop I've been told about.

Amazing it is. I walk away a few hundred dollars poorer but in possession of a super-sexy, super low-cut one-piece bathing suit. Todd has a hot tub and now I am ready!

I also make a quick pit stop at the local market. I reckon that even though Todd will be cooking dinner, I'll make my famous artichoke-asiago dip as a starter. The one that everyone raves about. The one that people beg me to bring to parties. The one that I'm told I should mass market. What better way to impress a new guy than with one of my signature creations? The way to a man's heart and all that.

I am more than ready when Todd comes home from work. Fully ensconced in his kitchen I am, with candle lit, wine poured and artichoke dip and fresh baguette just waiting to be sampled. And adored.

Dear Todd (who is actually quite cute in that older-dude kinda way) lays a huge grin on me (might have something to do with my plunging neckline) and gives me a quick hug. Then he takes one look at my dazzling dip and says in the flattest tone imaginable, "What is *that*?"

Now it's my turn to grin. "That is my world-famous asiago-artichoke dip!"

"I thought *I* was cooking dinner?" he whispers icily.

"I know, and of course you are," I continue to chirp merrily. "I just thought we could have this artichoke dip as a starter."

Todd glares at me like he has only just realized I have two heads. "I don't eat artichokes."

Not "Wow, Vickie, that looks smashing and so do you but I'm not really an artichoke fan" or go ahead, lie you putz and just say "I'm allergic to artichokes and will die a horrible mouth-frothing death before your very eyes if I so much as sniff one!"

Nope. He just plain doesn't eat 'em. No reason. Doesn't wanna.

Artichicken.

Our date goes downhill from there. Todd ignores my creation completely (even the bread!). He sets out to barbecue some chicken and instructs me to head to the beach. Solo.

"What? You're not coming with me to see the sunset?" *What the heck kind of date is this?*

"No Vickie, I am not. I have some cooking to do here and besides, I've seen that sunset a million times. You really should see it for the first time on your own."

Well, thank you Mr. Romance! All my visions of a hand-in-hand stroll to the water's edge, tummies sated after some yummy dip, second best sunset in the whole fucking world just waiting for us before a romantic dinner cooked just for me — all those visions go up in smoke. Not only is Todd an artichicken, he is a romantic dud. I eat his dried-out barbecued chicken and overdressed salad. I drink lots of wine. We have a hot tub and, yes, I show off my new bathing suit. We do some kissing in that hot tub and it isn't horrible but it isn't life-changing either, and then Todd tucks me into that convenient main-floor bed. There will be no hanky-panky with Todd. That's his rule. No first night hanky-panky. He kisses me on the forehead and departs to his own boudoir, leaving me in the bed he has specifically arranged for first-nighters. How chivalrous.

I'm a little bleary-eyed first thing in the morning but not so much that I can't fully enjoy a new vision — Todd strutting around the kitchen in a terry cloth robe pulled down to his waist and tied tightly around his rather substantial girth. This is not a look even Brad Pitt should attempt so I'm not quite sure what Todd is thinking, but as he leans against the kitchen counter, slurping milky cereal from his plastic bowl with his gut naked for the world to see, all I can think is *he looks pregnant.*

We only have that one date. I fall in love with Southampton and return many times and I do run into Todd on occasion. But there is no Cupid's arrow for Todd and me. Romantic ineptitude and protruding belly aside, he is an artichicken! Enough said.

So here's the thing with artichokes: I'm not even exactly sure what a fresh one looks like. I sure as heck wouldn't know what to do with one. I only buy them in cans (not marinated in jars) and no-name brands are just fine. Okay? Here we go.

Artichoke-Asiago Dip

I always give credit where credit is due, the mark of a proud cheater, and the original recipe for this was given to me by that same ex-friend who now grows breadcrumbs in my ex-husband's kitchen. There is really only one huge difference between hers and mine — and trust me, huge it is. She combines all the ingredients in a blender or food processor or whatever those handy-dandy machines are that turn perfectly good peasant fare, you know — chunky and unrefined — into pablum. And that's the problem with every store-bought artichoke-asiago dip I've ever tried. Too creamy. Too processed. You can't taste the artichoke. Or the cheese for that matter. So unplug your appliances and get ready to chop!

---

1 can of artichokes, drained and chopped into small pieces (you decide!)

1/2 cup old white cheddar (the older the better but when I'm feeling cheap I use no-name)

2/3 cup asiago

3 tablespoons mayonnaise

whole bunch ground pepper

3 or 4 tsp. garlic (or if you want to be a princess go ahead and use real garlic — 3 or 4 cloves)

Mix it all together and refrigerate — the longer the better. Just before serving nuke it until it's warm but not scalding. The flavours really do "melt" together beautifully.

Serving suggestion: spoon it onto thin baguette slices and top with an apple wedge. Divine. If you're on a diet or gluten free just spoon the dip right onto the apple wedge — also divine!

Artichoke-Asiago Pizza

There are two ways to approach this one: the "leftover" way and the "start from almost scratch" way (please note I said *almost*). It depends on what's in your fridge.

The leftover way:

---

1 large flatbread or pizza crust

leftover artichoke-asiago dip (as above)

1/2 cup bits of spicy Italian sausage or bacon, chopped

big handful of fresh baby spinach

1/2 cup Parmesan, grated (if you're feeling overwhelmingly cheesy)

Spread the dip onto the crust, sprinkle on the sausage, top with spinach and Parmesan. Bake at 400F directly on the oven rack for 10-12 minutes, until the crust is golden. As a rule of thumb, always let pizza sit for a few minutes before cutting. It gives the crust a chance to firm up a bit (unlike my arms, which get rather jiggly the more I sit). And truly: invest in a really good pizza cutter. This is one instance where a knife just won't cut it (pun intended).

If there's no dip left over from last night's party and your desire for artichokes is still unquenched, try this:

The "start from almost scratch" way:

---

1 can artichokes, drained and chopped

2 tablespoons pesto from a jar (yes, I know some people make pesto from scratch when they're not busy with breadcrumbs, but I am not one of said people)

1/2 cup asiago, grated

1/2 cup white cheddar, grated (or mozzarella or Parmesan or even just more asiago!)

1/2 cup spicy Italian sausage or bacon, chopped

handful of fresh baby spinach

Spread the pesto onto the crust (I like to use a brush but a spoon will do), lay out the artichokes, sprinkle on the cheese and sausage, top with spinach. Bake at 400F directly on the oven rack for 10-12 minutes, until the crust is golden. And don't worry if you're not a fan of cooked (wilted) spinach on pizza, just don't use it. If you are a fan remember that spinach really reduces when cooked, so don't be afraid to pile on tons! The other option is to put fresh spinach on top AFTER you've baked the pizza. Arugula also works.

I must give large credit to my ex-lover's ex-wife who is my ex-husband's current lover. This dip has become a vital part of my culinary repertoire. It's nice to know that something good came out of all the torment. I mean something besides the fact that my ex-husband and my ex-lover's wife seem really happy together. And it's been sixteen years!

Lettuce Entertain You

ONE OF THE MOST IMPRESSIVE CREATIONS YOU CAN ADD TO YOUR CULINARY REPERTOIRE IS HOMEMADE SALAD DRESSING. And if I may toot my own horn for a sec, this one is also "from scratch." Are you impressed yet?

Kidding. There are only three ingredients so Gordon Ramsay doesn't have to fret. But this one really does impress. And salad dressing ain't rocket science. At least not this one. It's my personal favourite and you'll find it used throughout this book on everything from pasta to fish to — ohmygosh — actual salads. This one is such a big hit with the folks who dine at my kitchen counter, I whipped up a cauldron of it one Christmas, poured it into dollar store glass bottles, stuck on sparkly labels and curly bows and voila! homemade Christmas gifts. You would have thought I had given them diamonds. I am no Martha Stewart, I assure you. I don't do crafts. I once offered to pay someone to do my scrapbook page at a bridal shower. I can barely sew on a button and there are no handmade ornaments on my Christmas tree. So this salad dressing/gift was HUGE! And reasonably cheap, I might add.

It was also my first source of post-marital culinary pride. I had previously been a confirmed dressing-off-the-shelf-buyer. Until my competition gene kicked in. You know the one? The one that screams "Anything Hubby's new girlfriend can do, I can do better!" And yes, that chick is a master of a simple oil and vinegar which, as it turns out, is my husband's favourite. I was determined to take it a step further.

So here we go. And please be forewarned, you are about to enter the land of "WTF?" I rarely use measuring cups or spoons or other mathematical devices designed to guarantee perfection. I use my eye, my tongue and my intuition. Not necessarily in that order.

Damn. Cooking and life are so similar.

We'll start with a small batch just in case my calculations are way off. What? I'm supposed to test this stuff? Ha! Let's just hope for the best.

Orange-Mango Salad Dressing

1/2 cup citrus olive (or grapeseed) oil

This used to be a lot harder to find but lately it's been getting easier, even at the local chain grocery store. Lemon olive oil from President's Choice is a simple find. But I will admit gourmet shops are great for this one — lots of choices and SO worth the extra expense. My favourite is orange and I recently discovered a company called ZOE (out of Montreal) who will deliver right to your door!

Okay, ready for a detour? You can also infuse your own oil. I've done it and it works. I actually prefer grapeseed oil because it is lighter tasting and still good for you. I take half a bottle, add orange zest (you know, just use your cheese grater and grate the peel off the fruit) and squeeze in a bit of the juice. Then shove in a few pieces of the orange and let it sit. Forever. Or a few weeks. How do you reckon those secretive Italians do it? Actually I have no idea, but this works for me.

1/2 cup mango vinegar

Also not leaping off the shelf at every market, but ZOE has this too. If you're not in the ordering mood, here's your cheat: buy any old mango or citrus dressing. No-name, brand name, marinade, dipping sauce, nectar — anything liquid that tastes like mangoes. Here's why: the very word "mango" impresses people. *She cooks with mango? Oh my.*

dump it all into a wide-mouthed salad dressing bottle

I have a very cool one with a cork, recycled from some expensive dressing I bought before I embraced cheating, but even a mason jar — or any jar — will do. Dump, shake, and then grind a whole bunch of pepper into it. I love that term "whole bunch." I use it all the time in cooking. I also use "tiny bit" and "handful" and I hope you will too. Whole bunch. Tiny bit. Handful. Whatever you think is the right amount. Taste it (dip in a piece of lettuce) and you'll know. It is all about *you* after all.

Good. Well done. It can now sit on your kitchen counter for weeks (no refrigeration required but if you used store-bought citrus dressing you'll probably want to), impressing all who notice. And there you have it, my new gourmand. EPLS (easy-peasy-lemon-squeezy) homemade mango-citrus salad dressing. If you infused your own oil it took two weeks and two minutes. If you didn't, two minutes. You're already a star!

Cheater Tip!

While we're on the subject, here's another tip to fool the world into thinking you know what you're doing: line up all your oils and vinegars somewhere prominently in the kitchen. Mine are on an open shelf. I mean, come on, they are right there where you can access them instantly because you are after all — a chef! You must be good!

Ready for another? If you're one of those creamy salad dressing girls — and who isn't at least sometimes? — try this little cheat. It's especially yummy on mushroom/spinach salad or even tuna salad:

1/2 cup Hidden Valley Ranch dressing (the best, in my humble opinion)

1/4 cup balsamic vinegar

whole bunch of pepper

Let's call this one Balsamic Ranch.

Yes, I know: how does she do it? The cleverness, the wit! It's why they pay me the big bucks on radio. Okay, the bucks aren't that big. But I do get to talk for a living!

Oh yeah — did I mention that I host a radio show? Remember that day job I spoke about? I used to do the midday show on a smooth jazz station, WAVE 94.7. For eleven years it was a pretty cushy gig because I pre-recorded (*voice-tracked* in radio lingo) all my shows. Thanks to modern technology I could blast through a five-hour show in twenty minutes which meant I only had to go to work one day a week. It didn't matter where I lived, as long as I could get to the station one day a week I was golden. I would record seven shows back-to-back, bingo/bango, lay down a few commercials and then go home. All in one day. I loved it!

Alas, all good things do come to an end and my beloved jazz station flipped to country. Hee haw. Not all bad though, because the owners of my station love smooth jazz as much as I do and they opted to keep us alive online at www.wave.fm. I am now the morning host, on the air seven days a week. The even better news is they set me up to record from home, which is mind-bogglingly brilliant. No more winter commutes and no more marathon recording sessions. I have been told it takes a certain crazy brain to blast through thirty or more hours of programing in one sitting. And now, recording every day, I don't have to. I can be as topical as you like. And yes, still a little crazy.

I also have an occasional evening job. I sing jazz. And I dabble in blogging (winesoakedramblings.com), social media support and teaching yoga (more on that coming up). But whether employed full-time or not, I realize that most people simply don't have the time or energy to build meals from scratch. Which is why cheating makes so much sense.

So yeah, Balsamic Ranch. It's a winner. Clever me, right? Okay maybe not so clever with salad dressing names but clever enough to write the script seven years in a row for the Canadian Smooth Jazz Awards. What a treat that was! Putting words (funny ones, I hope) into everyone's mouth, dressing up fancy, meeting all the smooth

jazz stars, presenting an award and even winning one the first year —
Broadcaster of the Year. I reckon because I was the only broad in the
category. Whatever the reason, it was a life highlight and a night I'll
never forget.

Salad Days

OKAY, SO NOW YOU'VE GOT YOUR SHOW-OFF HOMEMADE SALAD DRESSINGS READY TO, WELL, SHOW OFF. But on what? Gee, since it is called salad dressing, let's start with salads. But be forewarned, we will use this stuff on fish and pasta too!

When I was a kid, there were basically two kinds of salads: iceberg lettuce with tomatoes and maybe some cucumber if we were feeling frisky. Or coleslaw. Ho-hum.

Salads are now signature events in my kitchen. My pal and guitar player, Jose, actually cried the one time he came to dine and I neglected to make a salad. Okay, seriously, no he did not shed tears. He is a grown man after all (except for those moments when he used to whine about *his* love life) but he does rave about my greens. Much like Shayann says my kitchen is the best restaurant in town, Jose says I am the best salad maker on the planet. I accept these words of high praise with huge gratitude and make a salad almost every night.

With salads as anything else, there are no hard and fast rules. I simply experiment and taste and add and modify until the flavours all mesh beautifully.

And I'm never afraid to ask. I am the nosiest restaurant diner of all time. I ask waiters, the chef (I've wandered into the odd kitchen), the maître d', even the people sitting at the table next to me. One time I was at a five-star restaurant just about orgasmic over the garlic mashed potatoes. When the couple next to me could no longer ignore my moans of delight, I insisted they dip their spoons into my personal plop of potato and sample for themselves. It was becoming a veritable orgy. Then they let me taste their personal polenta plop and by the end of the meal we were exchanging recipes and emails. So go ahead — be nosy. It's how you'll learn.

When I say there are no hard and fast rules for salads what I really mean is you don't have to do anything — heck, it's *your* kitchen — but I think most everyday salads should include the following:

*cut up fruit

My favourites: clementines, mangoes, cantaloupe, blueberries, navel orange wedges.

Not bad: pears, nectarines, peaches.

Not so great: apples (unless it's a Waldorf, see below) because they tend to go brown quickly, strawberries or raspberries (too mushy — save those for dessert!), kiwi (spongy), watermelon (too seedy), grapefruit (too sour), plums (just wrong) and bananas (just gross).

Dried fruit is also good, especially cranberries and mangoes (are you detecting a major mango theme here?).

*nuts

When I'm feeling completely decadent I use candied cashews. Or butter toffee almonds. Anything sugary sweet. Your salad becomes dessert!

For every day I go with cashews, almonds or walnuts.

*cheese

I love feta (crumbled) or goat cheese (try the cranberry or pepper kind and warm it up in the microwave first — the flavours really burst).

Asiago is awesome (especially combined with arugula — see below).

Plain old cheddar will always do. Actually, any kind of cheese will always do.

*fennel (or anise)

This is my not-so-secret ingredient and I guarantee it will turn an ordinary salad into a "Wow - this is amazing!" experience. That slight hint of licorice – mmm - yummy!

Before we get to some actual salad recipes, just a few rules. Now you already know I'm not a fan of rules so let's just call them "suggestions." You see, rules and I have never been simpatico. I've actually lived most of my life by the credo "It's easier to ask forgiveness than permission." Naturally this has led to the occasional spot of trouble — like the time when I was about nine and I wanted to make a caramel apple (it was right after Halloween) but my parents weren't home so I broke the "no cooking when we're not here" rule. I unwrapped the caramels and put them on the stove to melt...in a plastic cottage cheese container because, golly, it seemed to be about the right size. And melt they did. While I completely forgot about my cooking project, engrossed in after-school television as I was, the entire mess melted unceremoniously into the coil burner. Yes, that was a day when asking for forgiveness figured huge in my life.

Cheater Tips!

1. Never put tomatoes and fruit in the same salad. I know that sounds weird since a tomato is apparently a fruit (and how dumb is that?) but to my taste there is something strangely contradictory about tangy tomatoes next to sweet fruits. You will get a certain amount of juice from both so those juices better have a nice blend. I mean really, ever heard of an orange tomato smoothie? Mango tomato yogurt? Tomato clementine sorbet? They just don't go together.

2. Always under-dress a salad. I can't stand a salad drowning in dressing, even if it is my homemade mango-citrus delight. I want to taste the lettuce, the fruit, the cheese — everything. Not just the sauce. If you're serving a dress-aholic (you know who you are!) just put a little extra on the table. Let them drown their own. And always dress your salad just before serving. You don't want it to get all wilty and dressing-logged. Oh, one other thing about dressing: I really feel it needs to be tossed into the salad, not just drizzled on top. When you drizzle and don't toss, everything underneath is dry and everything on top is soggy. So toss! Invest in a huge salad bowl too, so that you are tossing in the container and not all over the table.

3. Don't put too many ingredients into one salad. Once you've got your greens, fruit, cheese, nuts and fennel you're pretty well covered. If you start adding carrots, cucumber, celery, broccoli, macaroni and lima beans the tastes will just get all jumbled up. Save those for a different salad. Go ahead — be creative! Invent lots of interesting salads. Just don't put them all in the same bowl at the same time.

4. Don't ever buy iceberg lettuce again. It tastes like nothing and it's not even that good for you. Go dark green. Spinach, arugula and romaine are my staples. Spring mix, mesclun mix, Italian mix, any of those pre-washed ready-to-go bags are good too.

Okay, ready? A few basic salads you may want to try before you venture off on your own salad days.

The Drive-Your-Company-Crazy Salad

> **whole bunch of baby spinach** (fill 2/3 of the bowl)
>
> **smaller bunch of arugula** (it's spicy and gives the salad a somewhat nutty flavour)
>
> **1 stalk of fennel,** chopped into bite-size pieces I use both the bulb and the stem. My ex-boyfriend, Grover – the one I cheated with and yes I just made up that name (to protect the guilty) but it seems somehow appropriate — even tossed in the leafy bits at the top. Then he tossed me (more on that later)
>
> **one ripe mango,** peeled and cut into morsels
>
> **1/2 cup feta cheese,** crumbled
>
> **1/4 cup dried cranberries**
>
> **1/3 cup candied cashews**
>
> **citrus-mango dressing** Here I would love to say "to taste" but I know that for some of you that is far too daunting. But just for now because soon, as you get the hang of this, it won't be. I'm going to say 1/4 cup (if it's typically a big salad bowl)

Mix all the ingredients together and remember to put the dressing on just before serving. Don't forget to toss (the salad, not me or your boyfriend, unless of course it's time)!

Simple-Yet-Elegant Arugula Salad

This one is a prime example of how very few ingredients can make a big impression. It's not for sissies — you've got to love the bold flavour of arugula (also called "rocket") and the piquant taste of the cheese.

whole bunch of arugula (fill the bowl)

whole bunch — okay, maybe 1/2 cup — asiago, grated Get the aged, crumblier kind because there is also a cheap, spongy type which is a huge disappointment. Costco is perfect for this.

citrus-mango dressing — maybe 1/4 cup You really want to under-dress this one because arugula gets very wilty very fast. Add a dash (maybe a teaspoon?) of balsamic vinegar and a bit (1/2 tsp.) of sugar and shake it up, baby. You will get a sweet bit of zing and your friends will think you've invented a whole new salad dressing, you talented thing, you

Spicy Spinach Mushroom Salad

It's the classic spinach/mushroom combo — with some "zoom"!

whole bunch of baby spinach (2/3 of the bowl)

1 cup of cremini mushrooms In my opinion they have more taste than plain white ones but you can use any kind of mushroom you want

dash Montreal steak spice

1 Tbsp. butter

2 hard-boiled eggs

1/4 cup spicy Italian sausage, chopped

1/4 cup Balsamic Ranch dressing

Sauté the mushrooms in butter or garlic oil. At some point, as they brown, crank the heat to high (don't walk away!) and let them actually almost burn a little bit. They will caramelize and get even yummier. At this stage, toss in the Montreal steak spice. What a marvelous invention it is! Just be careful with amounts — too much spice and all you'll taste is salt.

Remove the mushrooms from the pan, set aside to cool and fry up that sausage, which you have chopped into the teensiest morsels possible. I know, most people put bacon in a salad like this, but this sausage will make you a star. It kicks. And gets crunchy like bacon when you fry it long enough, which isn't long at all. I've actually nuked it when I was in a hurry but if you do, be careful — it can get kind of splatty in your microwave.

Chop up the hard-boiled eggs you have presumably boiled already, thus the name hard-boiled. Put it all together, dress before serving and dig in!

PS: For added crunch, toss in 1/2 cup of chopped celery, red onion or grated carrots.

Waldorf Euphoria Salad

> **whole bunch of romaine lettuce** (2/3 of the bowl)
>
> **1/2 cup celery,** chopped
>
> **2 apples** Your choice, but I love Honey Crisp. Peeled or not (your choice again but I will tell you I rarely peel apples or pears or peaches or nectarines because I am LAZY!), cut into bite-size pieces
>
> **1/2 cup walnuts,** chopped
>
> **1/4 cup Balsamic Ranch dressing**

Mix the romaine, celery and walnuts. Add the apples and dressing just before serving. Easy-peasy-lemon-squeezy and very sweet!

And one more PS regarding salads: You'll notice I never use croutons. And I absolutely love bread. It's because I absolutely love bread that I choose not to put it into my salads. I would rather save my bread calories for fresh bread consumption, not old toast in greens.

To me it doesn't add enough taste to justify the calories. But that's just me. If you want old toast in your salads, go crazy! And if you want to make croutons from scratch just **cut up an old, dried-up Ace baguette and fry it up in President's Choice garlic oil** (another staple in my pantry). **Add salt and pepper** and there you go — you've magically grown your own croutons!

Artichokes, Asiago and Autonomy

YOU MAY HAVE NOTICED BY NOW THAT I AM INCAPABLE OF MENTIONING ARTICHOKES WITHOUT ASIAGO. These two tasty victuals (don't you just love that word?) just go together like peanut butter and jam, macaroni and cheese, red wine and dark chocolate (is that just me?). I simply cannot have one without the other. Okay, that's a lie. I am perfectly capable of drinking red wine without chocolate and I've been known to eat chocolate long before the cocktail hour begins. And truth be told, I don't even like jam. But you get my point.

This easy-peasy pasta dish is something I invented soon after my marriage broke up. My ex-husband really is a fabulous guy, a wonderful son and brother, even better son-in-law (I'm pretty sure my mother liked him more than she liked me), a loyal friend and an attentive and loving father. What he was not (please note I say *was* because things changed post-split in a most resounding way) was *emotionally available*. Even, ultimately, by his own admission.

Still, immediately after I left, I was spending about twenty hours a day weeping buckets of guilt and despair while still visiting the marital home for several hours each day, ostensibly to cook and do laundry but really to weep those buckets in his presence. I was desperate for forgiveness. Absolution. Understanding. HBS was actually quite lovely through it all. Kind, caring and even a bit philosophical.

Him: "Vickie, for crying out loud, stop crying all the time!"

Me: snivel, snivel, wail, moan, almost hyper-ventilate.

Him: "Seriously Vickie, it's okay. I know this is killing you. It's killing me too. But please get a grip! Remember that in a hundred years we will all be dust and none of this will matter anyway. Just go find a jewel in every single day and hang on to that."

Such a poet. And he would hug me while I sniveled and moaned some more. I know, right? This is the guy I cheated on and then left for another man. Sometimes I still shake my head.

Yes, great guy and also a really great cook. But the thing is, his palate was somewhat limited. He was not big on spicy (unless it's hot sauce on a taco) and he was not terribly adventuresome. I'm pretty sure he and Todd would see eye to eye on the whole artichoke thing. His idea of a perfect meal was white rice with lots of soya sauce, a piece of grilled meat and a veg. Maybe a salad but only lettuce and tomatoes, if you please. There'd be a full roast beef dinner on Sundays and I will tell you the man makes the best roast potatoes and Yorkshire pudding — from scratch (ouch)!

So, I don't think he'd care much for this pasta. Perhaps that is why I created it? I cooked for him all those years we were married. Dinner was pretty much the only time we interacted, so I wanted him to be happy. And he was. At least about the food. I can't remember a night when he didn't finish off by saying, "Thank you, my darling, that was wonderful." As a budding chef, you know how much those words mean. As a wife, even more so. But as a frustrated diner, I never found my palate.

I'm not insinuating that I cheated on my husband because we only hung out at dinner time and preferred different foods. I doubt he and his current roommate are always on the same culinary page either. What they have in common that we didn't is...things in common. They both like to garden. I have a purple thumb. My idea of gardening is placing a pre-potted geranium into a lovely urn. They both ride motorcycles. I hate helmet-head. They both nest happily. I am an incorrigible gypsy and could move every second year (and have!). Neither of them has an overwhelming need to over-analyze every emotional droplet of agony that oozes from their pores on a daily basis. Because unlike me and my damn stupid pores, it doesn't. Their pores are quite content to remain ooze-less. HBS and Kay are simpatico. I believe they meet each other's needs quite handily.

HBS and I were reasonably contented friends who shared a certain intellectual harmony but in the department of emotion and passion we failed miserably. Much like with our palates, he was comfortable with plain and I was longing for fire. Unfortunately I never found it. Truth be told I most likely didn't find it because I had no idea how to work towards it. Or on it. Or with him for it. Much like our dinner menu, it was so much easier to keep things simple. Status quo. No boat-rocking and no fire-starting.

But on this particular evening in my new single-woman townhouse kitchen, I was all alone. I was blasting music and burning candles — yes, even just for me. And so I decided to create something new and special *for me*. Something I would enjoy. Who cares about dumb boys?

Well actually, I did. You see, that dumb boy Grover, he of adorable good looks, wicked smile and instant love-of-my-life status, was still in the picture at that moment. Ultimately he would dump me not once but FOUR times! But at this moment we were into Round #2 of our relationship and he was coming for dinner.

But this wasn't about him. It was about me cooking for me.

So I started to chop. Chopping, slicing, dicing, it's all therapy for me. I'm pretty sure Grover and I were on the rocks because we were almost always on the rocks, one of the nasty side effects that accompanies cheating, guilt and remorse. So there I was, inventing and healing all at the same time.

Okay, this is where I should probably tell you a bit more about that big, aforementioned, adventuresome, non-cooking cheating misstep. See, as you may have by now surmised, at one time Grover was actually married to Kay, the girl who cooks from scratch and grows breadcrumbs. When we met they were seemingly happily married (to each other) and so was I (to fabulous Yorkshire pudding man). Seemingly. Yes, I had felt a powerful attraction to Grover that very first evening, but I was an accomplished hider. Under carpet sweeper. My husband and I did it all the time. It took effort but hey, I got my degree in drama. I am a perfectly capable actress and I was perfectly capable of pretending to like Kay every bit as much as I liked her husband. Maybe more.

The thing is I really did like Kay. She is funny and warm and loving. Her only downside was that marriage license. I chose to ignore that pesky hindrance (and my attraction to her husband) and we all became pals. We started hanging out. We had lots of fun times together.

We shared dinner parties and Jam sessions. We went camping and canoeing. We cottaged together and cooked together. We became besties!

The trouble started when, fifteen months after that initial meeting, Grover and I fell in love. Yes, it's always troublesome to fall in love with someone else's husband when you have a perfectly good one of your own and the wife of said other husband is someone you actually like.

Really troublesome.

I knew from day one, even moment one, that I was way too attracted to Grover. He is witty, engaging, feisty and illegally cute. And right from the get-go he seemed very interested in interacting with me. We enjoyed verbal sparring and we made each other laugh. A lot. You know how compelling that is? Particularly when your matrimonial interaction is limited to dinner time, typically shared with Vanna and Pat from *Wheel of Fortune.*

I back-burnered every illicit feeling and fantasy for those fifteen months. Even as we all grew increasingly close, I convinced myself that it was just a crush. Nothing would ever come of my folly. I was perfectly able to keep my secret feelings for Grover fully under control. Kay seemed particularly interested in forging a friendship with me, which would have been great except for her husband and those darned illicit feelings. Still, he knew nothing of them. He liked hanging out with HBS, and Kay and I shared occasional girl time. Sometimes it was natural, other times uncomfortable (for me). But we were in it. I never believed we were heading toward a cliff.

But we were.

In the tiniest increments, the precipice got closer and closer. It wasn't just me and my secret anymore. Grover suddenly seemed in on it. And open to it. Neither of us was exactly sure when we crossed the line. All I know is Grover and I soon found ourselves with our four unmarried (to each other) feet dangerously dangling.

Emails meant to be purely logistical turned into flirt fests. Friendly kisses on the cheek became overly friendly lip-locks. Therapeutic shoulder massages became sensual caresses. Stolen glances filled with anticipation and promise became routine. This all built up to the fateful day when he called our home, ostensibly to speak with my husband who, as it turns out, was not there. So there we were, just the two of us, alone with nothing separating us but a phone line and two old promises. The time had come. Our ardour could no longer simmer unaddressed.

"Be careful, Grover." I was speaking very slowly with determination. At that moment there were so many words I wanted desperately to hear and so many words I was absolutely terrified of hearing. "Because whatever you say next could irrevocably alter the course of seven lives. Irrevocably."

Seven lives. Four spouses and three children (they have two daughters). I wasn't even considering the ripple effect at that moment. All I knew was that seven lives would change dramatically.

He said it anyway. "I have these feelings for you, Vickie," he stammered helplessly. "Feelings I know I shouldn't have but they are there and they are real and I cannot hold this in a moment longer. I need you to know. And I need to know if I'm just imagining this or fantasizing this or dreaming this or do you have these feelings too?"

It was a mind-blowing, soul-affirming, heart-exploding moment. After so much time and so much buried longing, to actually feel this man's affection in all its agonizing glory was beyond my wildest dreams.

And my absolute worst fucking nightmares.

Didn't matter. The train had left the station.

I paused for as long as I could, breathing heavily, heart constricted, knowing that I could stop this all with a word.

"Yes."

In hindsight, not the most prudent word. But it was the only word I could find. Because it was the truth. And I was so very tired of lying.

"I need to see you. Alone."

More magic words from him.

And so we arranged a private moment.

The following evening Grover would come to our home early for a music rehearsal. We had put together a little band for our neighbour's twenty-fifth anniversary party; yes those very same friends who had introduced us a lifetime ago. Grover played harmonica, HBS played guitar, I was the lead singer and band chief. There were others involved but this would be our first practice, where we would determine repertoire. Just the three of us.

"Tomorrow." I managed to croak out one word.

"Tomorrow?" he responded with obvious hope in his voice.

"Tomorrow. Come early for rehearsal. My husband will be out fetching Jack from an after-school party. Just show up early. You know, like, innocently."

Innocently my ass.

Grover did exactly as requested. He wasn't interested in innocence anymore either.

I remember those moments before he arrived like it's a movie I have watched over and over again. I was at the piano, singing a Stevie Wonder song called *Lately*, in which he suspects his lover is cheating. I was feeling sick to my stomach, lamenting my wonderful husband and his blissful ignorance. Streams of tears cascaded down my cheeks as I tried to sing the song.

What the hell are you thinking, Vickie? I admonished myself harshly. You will not do this. You absolutely will not.

I truly believed this one-woman conference would do the trick. I was sad but determined. Resigned. Romantic dreams would not come true, no sir, not on my watch. I would send that damn train back. HBS did not deserve this and neither did Grover's wife.

"Hello???"

I heard his voice as he opened the downstairs door.

One deep breath filled with all the resolve I could muster and down the stairs I flew. Straight into his arms and the most ardent, passionate, fulfilling kiss I had ever experienced in my entire forty-eight years. It was like he was the only man I had ever kissed. The only man I had ever wanted to kiss. The only man I would ever kiss again.

And then he pulled back, took my face in his hands and whispered, "You are so beautiful."

I cannot emphasize what a monster moment that was. Because in all the thirteen years I was married, my husband never once told me I was beautiful. When I got all decked out he told me I looked good, or nice or lovely. He might comment on my attractive outfit. He might just nod approval. But not once did he say the word beautiful.

Grover and I continued kissing and holding each other and touching each other and talking and kissing. I had no control, no resolve and no conscience. I was exactly where I wanted to be.

"I know what we are doing is wrong but I can't stop and I don't want to stop," I mumbled between mouthfuls of passion. "I want this. I want you. I want to be with you for real. Forever. As soon as possible."

He pulled back but kept a tight hold on my hands. "What are you saying, Vickie?"

I knew exactly what I was saying. "What I am saying is that I am willing to leave my marriage tonight. This very minute. Before anything more than a kiss has transpired. I do not want to cheat. I do not want to lie. I want to be with you for real and I am so ready to damn the torpedoes!"

"Okay now, baby, hold on." Oh how I loved that he called me baby. Not "honey baby sweetie" (tongue in cheek). Just baby. I wasn't crazy about the next sentence though. "We need to think about this. Figure it out. Plan it wisely."

He kissed me again, and again I was lost.

Before we knew it HBS retuned with our son and the discussion of future plans was placed on hold. That evening there were more stolen glances and furtive stares. Even a borrowed kiss or two when we were left alone. And thus began the first official night of our "affair."

Ah, the beauty of hindsight rears its ugly head. If I could do this all over again, dear reader, I would have stopped everything before my husband returned. I would have said to Grover firmly with complete resolve, "Call me when you're ready." I had cheated before. I truly did not want to do it again. Yes, I think I already knew that cheating was the easy way out. You want insta-passion and fireworks? Have an affair. You'll get it all in spades. But those spades are cheap and short-lived. They ultimately leave you feeling dirty and spent. I knew that big love and true passion demanded honesty. Maybe even work.

But there I was in the throes of unimaginable ecstasy. Except I had imagined it. And now it was happening. For real. And I wanted that passion far more than I wanted to be strong in my resolve. Resolve is usually in short supply when hearts and libidos are racing. Especially mine.

Grover and I endured nine inglorious months of lies, cheating (the bad kind), desperation and subterfuge. Ah yes, the subterfuge. It's incredible how creative a mind becomes when desire takes hold. There were certainly enough social occasions when sneaking off for a kiss was possible. It was those other private encounters that presented a challenge. But I can assure you desire always wins and we found ways. There were dalliances in my home on days he could sneak away from work running "errands." There were dalliances in the back of his work van when he could sneak away from work running errands and I could meet him. There were dalliances early in the morning when I walked the dog on the back trails and he pedaled furiously on his bicycle (ostensibly in an effort to get fit) and we would meet in the middle at a bench on a hilltop. Oh, the stories Katie, my dear mutt, could tell.

We once met at a farm he and his brother were renovating and had a lunchtime picnic in the barn, in the rain. We met in fields, parking lots and at the end of roads. We shared the lunch that his wife had lovingly packed for him more than once. I felt sick doing it and did it anyway. Because being with Grover was the only thing that mattered. I was consumed and obsessed and any attacks of conscience were easily squelched. All it took was his kiss. And we kissed a lot.

And then there was that time we rendezvoused in the dead of winter in the back seat of my jeep, parked at a deserted conservation area. A cop showed up and demanded an explanation.

"We're naked in here," I yelled through steamed-up windows, grateful that his view was inhibited. "Sorry sir," I added contritely, "but we're just trying to put a little spice back into our marriage."

The good cop laughed and wished us well, advising us as he departed to not freeze to death. Like I said, I'm a pretty good actress. Not necessarily a proud one. Just a good one. When I need to be.

During this time I travelled with HBS to visit his family overseas and Grover acted the dutiful husband at every turn. But there were several occasions when both our spouses raised an eyebrow. This was abject torture. And yet it went on and on. We had agreed to take a year to figure this out. And when I say *we* had agreed what I really mean is Grover asked for a year and I gave it to him. Reluctantly. But what choice did I have? I could either acquiesce or give him up. And giving him up was inconceivable.

Thus was born "The Agreement," written in longhand by Grover and delivered to me in secret:

The Agreement

I know this will be the longest year imaginuble. The longest.

We already know what we know. We already know how we feel.

We already know how to lie. We already know how to cry.

We already know what we want. And we know how much it hurts to not have it right now.

We also know how much it hurts to scheme and lie some more and fake our way through endless days.

But...I want you to write me the perfect song.

I want to get to know Jack and I want you to know my girls — before they hate us.

I want us to come up with some kind of plan that makes sense. There will be so much devastation and I want us to be ready.

Thank you for this agreement. We shook on it and I will do my part. I will keep scheming and lying and fighting back the tears that come far too frequently.

I will try my best not to lose my mind. Because I love you.

We were stupid in love, Grover and I, and even apart we stayed together via emails. This was before the days of texting and although we each had a cell phone and used them to communicate when we could, these emails became our poetry, a way to express our love and our fears and our desires in all those hours when being together was impossible. They were our lifeline and our loveline.

Our affair began in May and by July we were having trouble containing it. Neither of us had told anyone. It was our own private sacred jewel. And our own private sacred hell.

July 24 - From him:

> I feel the need to tell someone about us. But I don't know who. My brother? My brother-in-law? The clerk at Home Depot? I can't explain it. Maybe you've become such a big part of me you no longer fit inside my heart. What happens when you start to leak out?

July 28 - From her:

> When a woman is away from the man she loves...
>
> She cries in airplane bathrooms because she is watching a romantic comedy instead of living it.
>
> She buys keyboards in foreign lands so she can still sing his songs.
>
> She buys musical pins for all the boys in the band just so she can buy a special one for him.
>
> When a woman is away from the man she loves...
>
> She talks of him far too often and almost confesses her feelings to people who would probably rather not know.
>
> She starts to look at her husband like a warden.

She despairs at looking at her husband like a warden because he is not, and any prison is one of her own making and choosing.

When a woman is away from the man she loves...

She risks life and limb to check email in the hope that he may have found the opportunity to write a few lines (apparently some men do this too).

She writes him songs.

She smiles secretly at the memories.

When a woman is away from the man she loves, she longs for him with every breath.

She aches with anticipation.

Just as I ache for you right now, as any woman would, when she is away from the man she loves.

August 11 - From him:

Sundays are the worst. It's the one day I really want to be with you.

I miss you. I love you. I repeat these same six words every day. For some reason they hurt more on Sunday.

August 12 - From her:

More thunderstorms in the sky. Back again. Thunder and lightning and clouds full of rain. In my heart too. I miss you so much I could scream. How do I go a lifetime when I can't even go a day? Sometimes I feel like I'm typing into oblivion, never knowing if or when you will read these words. But at least they are meant for you.

My husband wants to talk. He is very suspicious. Of you, of me, of us. I want so badly to tell him the truth and get on with our future. And yet I know this is not what you want.

I don't know what to say. I don't know what to do.

August 21 - From him:

My dearest Vickie,

I am shaking with shame, knowing what is happening at your house.

I know how much I want to be with you. I can't imagine the unbearable pain of not being with you. Is this what your husband is thinking? Is this what I am so willing to cause?

And what about my wife? How do I tell her I am in love with someone else? How do we tell our children? Are we allowed to fuck up so many innocent lives because of our passion? Is our selfish love worth it?

I feel sick right now. I know you do too and I am so very sorry.

Signed,

Your coward

August 22 - From her:

Since yesterday afternoon I have written a thousand emails to you. All in my head. I have called you a coward, a saint, the love of my life and the reason I want to die. I have written you a poem, cursed your name, ached for you in a way I can't describe and longed with all my heart for an email. And now here it is.

I'm sorry you are shaking. But my heart is trembling too.

Here's what I know:

I love you. But I hate myself.

In the past 24 hours I have

- assured my husband that my flirtation with you is harmless, and in no way the cause of any problems in our marriage.

- admitted that there are many problems in our marriage, but when he offered that perhaps they were insurmountable and that we should seriously consider other options, I hummed and hawed and finally tap-danced my way back into his heart.

- held his hand, kissed his mouth and made love to him, all the while thinking of you.

- gardened, cut the grass, stewed tomatoes, cooked meals and tried to be a model wife.

I deserve a fucking Oscar but I can hardly look at myself in the mirror.

Your time has been bought. I can only hope the price is not too high.

August 24 - From her:

In spite of these past few days of angst and confusion, self-loathing and despair and every other heart-wrenching, melodramatic emotion I can muster...I love you. And it just occurred to me that the "I don't knows" might just be our penance. The divine retribution for our sins.

But today it all became very clear to me. I love you. And because I love you I don't want to torture you. I don't want to torture you with choices you cannot make, decisions you cannot live with and possible regret you cannot forgive. I am here for you in whatever way you want. Stolen moments, every moment, no moments... whatever you choose. I've said it before — your love is a gift. I accept it with all strings attached.

I am and will always remain...

Your girl.

August 25 - From him:

I know the truth. Even with all the hurt and sorrow it will cause I know the truth. The time will soon come that I can no longer stand being apart from you.

September 2 - From her:

The most wonderful thing you've ever said to me was last Friday at noon, when you told me you had thought about having a baby with me. I would do that and a whole lot more. Because of all the things I've said to you, the absolute truest is this — you are the love of my life. I've always known there is only one and I waited a long time to find you.

So whatever this is, it is. Whatever we are, and will be, is just that. Because you are who you are.

And I am your girl.

October 12 - From her:

A paraphrased quote from last night's episode of Everwood:

"For most of us, our fatal flaw is fear of change. No matter how much pain we are in right now, we fear even more the pain that we don't know..."

And then there was a health scare. Mine. Lumps on my thyroid. Tests, ultrasounds, nuclear medicine, all of us waiting to find out if I had cancer. HBS was surprisingly nonplussed. We were hosting a gathering of friends and I had escaped to the bathroom to have a cry. I guess he noticed my absence because he soon found me, sitting on the toilet seat, wiping away tears and dripping mascara.

"I'm scared." That's all I whimpered.

"Of what?" His tone was bordering on impatient.

"Of cancer!" I said. I actually wanted to say, "Of dying before I get to love Grover the way I want to love Grover!" but those words did not come out.

"Of course you don't have cancer, Vickie," he stated emphatically. "Stop worrying about it."

I reminded him that he had neglected to go to medical school and all these doctors had other opinions, but he would have none of that. He simply took my hand, pulled me to my feet, gave me a quick hug and suggested I clean up my face and return to our party. That was HBS. If there's a carpet close by, please sweep.

But not Grover. Grover was sick with worry and despair.

October 27 - From him:

> *I am once again filled with shame. I know you needed so much more from me yesterday. I know you are afraid. I am afraid too. Afraid that something will happen to prevent our dreams from coming true. Afraid for our mortality. Afraid that I will never find the courage to speak my truth and break so many hearts. And yet I know it is inevitable. You and I are inevitable. Our love is a wondrous gift and I realize now my sanity hinges on its fulfillment.*
>
> *I am ashamed I cannot move faster. Please forgive me.*

Thankfully, HBS was right. I had benign tumours, not cancer. At least not yet. I was told to return to the specialist if a large goiter ever appeared on my neck. So far, so good.

The emails continued ...

October 31 - From her:

> *The most wonderful things you've ever said to me:*
>
> *I love you.*
>
> *I've been thinking about having a baby with you.*
>
> *You're my favourite singer.*
>
> *Would you mind marrying me?*

Two in one morning? No wonder it was so amazing. Thank you for all of the above...and then some.

November 3 - From him:

It's getting dangerous, isn't it? Being together around so many other people. It scares me how dangerous it could be. But when you sang last night, all my fears disappeared. All I could hear were the words I knew you were singing for me.

And then I read your email and I am incredulous that these beautiful words are meant for me. Every day more and more of me belongs to you. And even though I am such a fucking mess, I love you.

Yep. We were insatiable. Burning with love. It's incredible how stolen love burns so much brighter than that run-of-the-mill everyday married kind.

Over these months of clandestine encounters and emotionally charged correspondence, Grover and I both became very fit and firm. No one questioned our new-found aerobic zeal. The dog's lips were sealed and all that walking and running, combined with my inability to eat much due to ongoing stress, led to my eventual 30 lb. weight loss. I call it the trauma diet and trust me, in spite of the workout and my new dress size, it's one I will never recommend.

Christmas was coming and we had still not been caught. I think we were actually getting a bit more brazen with our affection and yet HBS and Kay seemed fine. Sure, they had their suspicious moments but for the most part they were silent. We were socializing as couples more than ever and even getting merrily festive all together.

December 2 - From him:

> *I love seeing you. I love when you are here. I love watching you smile. I hate not being able to touch you. I hate not being able to kiss you. I miss you Vickie.*

December 3 - From her:

> *Yesterday afternoon I lay in bed for an hour fighting back tears.*
>
> *Then I cleaned the house and did laundry, fighting back tears.*
>
> *I drank a glass of wine, cooked dinner and shed a tear or two into the pork.*
>
> *Without even the tiniest amount of spirit, I listened to Christmas music and decorated our tree.*
>
> *I was forced to abandon the movie we were watching in order to go weep in the hot tub under a moonlit sky. After which I was forced to go straight to bed in order to hide my puffy eyes.*
>
> *Now here I am this morning, reading your email and weeping again.*
>
> *I want so much to love you with all of my heart. But I am so damn afraid to give you all of my heart because I am so damn afraid that one day you will annihilate it. And me.*

Oh, how very astute I was, even when I didn't realize it and certainly did not want my predictions to come true.

And then — the leaking began in earnest. I had already confessed to two long-time girlfriends. They both lived in other countries so I felt confident they would A) keep my secret and B) not feel guilty every time they looked at my husband because they never saw him. But Grover had told no one. I knew this was extremely difficult for him and I had a feeling that all the family festivities we were both experiencing, apart and together, would push him over the edge. And I wondered who he would tell first.

December 21 - From him:

> You said your gut was telling you that I was going to crack. Tell someone. Confess. Smart gut you have.
>
> I'm not sure if I can ever tell my wife but I told my brother. His response: "Holy Fuck!"

Christmas came and went with an overabundance of repressed emotion and suffocating guilt and yet we still managed to share the holiday spirit together with our families. Christmas Eve was at his house, Christmas Day at ours. A last-minute New Year's Eve celebration with friends allowed us the opportunity to share a special midnight kiss right after we kissed our spouses. We found ways to sit next to one another at dinners, rub toes under tables, sneak glances at parties and kisses in the kitchen.

How no one in our vast circle of friends and relatives ever guessed our secret is still beyond me. We were quickly losing our resolve to honour "The Agreement" and our sense of discretion diminished hourly. The new year dawned and Grover and I could not contain our feelings any longer.

January 7 - From her:

> This afternoon while driving home from work I called your wife. To talk about her poor ailing mother. We talked

for quite a while, she was very upset, and as I was pulling into the driveway she really started to cry. My heart was breaking. And after I hung up the phone I could feel her pain so profoundly I started to cry too.

And then I thought — If I can't even stand sharing her pain at the prospect of losing her mother, how could I ever cause her pain by telling her that I am in love with her husband? By asking her to understand that I need to be with him?

February 3 - From him:

My wife says I am inattentive. Non-communicative. Too involved with music and not involved enough with my family. She is right on all accounts. But what can I say? It's getting harder all the time to not tell her the truth.

February 8 - From him:

I am a coward, this I know. When the time comes to leave I will have to just go. Leave a note. Take a few things and sneak out the back door. I just cannot bear to watch. Whether she falls apart or tries to kill me. Doesn't matter. I cannot watch. Am I still your hero?

And then he told...his mother. Grover's parents are divorced but the whole darn family still lived more or less together. Together as in on the same "homestead." His dad lived in the original farmhouse. He, Kay and their daughters lived in the renovated barn on the same property. His mother lived next door in a house her boys built on land purchased from her ex-husband, and Grover's brother and his family lived in that home's main floor apartment. Have I lost you yet? Oh yeah, there's more. Grover and his brother run their renovating business out of a workshop beneath that same renovated barn. It's all very cozy.

I had met Grover's family on many occasions and found both his parents to be quite engaging. I had no idea how Anna would react but when Grover told her about me all she said was, "I'd like to talk with her." Wow.

He brought her over on a post-Christmas evening when both HBS and Jack were out. She just looked at me with her searing ice-blue eyes and said, "Do you love my son?"

I paused, looked at him, heart pounding. "He is the love of my life," I answered shakily.

She smiled. A beautiful smile that lit up those ice-blue eyes like lightning, rendering them identical to Grover's. "Then take care of him," she replied softly, "and I will take care of you both."

February 18 - From him:

> *Thank you. You showed my mother what is in your heart.*
> *And now she knows. Now she understands. Thank you.*

And then it came. Departure Eve. Or should I call it The Eve Before Explosion? We didn't know it at the time. On February 20, 2004, we two couples and many other mutual friends attended a fundraising dance for my son's school. Grover and I spent a lot of time together. Dancing. Examining the silent auction table. Eating dinner and dancing some more. People were watching and noticing and we didn't care. He was the magnet and I was steel.

On the following fateful evening, which happened be Grover and Kay's twenty-third wedding anniversary, we confessed and moved out. It wasn't exactly planned but it wasn't really a surprise (to us) either. We simply could not contain the truth amidst so much suspicion and speculation. HBS wanted answers. And I could not lie to my husband one more time. On that evening, he said to me somewhat cryptically,

"I think there will come a time very soon when you will have to choose between Grover and me." I didn't know exactly what he suspected but I did know the time had come. There would be no more carpet-sweeping and outright lying. The time had come for full disclosure, come what may. Grover knew I was going to confess and assured me that he too was prepared to leave.

And so I told HBS. In person. Simply and honestly I told him that I was in love with Grover and that our marriage was over. I told him that I loved him and always would but I was no longer in love with him. Yes, I know — standard drivel. But it was my truth.

Interestingly, Grover had suggested once that we withhold the full truth of our nine-month affair and confess only to "recently falling in love." He wanted to make us look a little less horrid, a little less duplicitous and perhaps a little more noble. Even though we were none of those things. I couldn't do it. I was exhausted from lying. And I did not want to start my new life with Grover with yet another untruth. So when HBS asked, I answered. Then I quietly got up and left the room.

I found Jack and told him too. I told him that much like he had once told me Grover was his favourite adult friend, he was also mine. I told him that grown-up love was impossible for an eleven-year-old to understand and I told him that I couldn't stay married to his father anymore. I told him that his father and I both loved him exactly as we always had and that we would continue to love him exactly as we always had. But that we would no longer all be together. I would be with Grover. Jack just started to cry. And then he left the room to find his father.

In the midst of my conversation with Jack, Kay called our house in a panic, wondering if I had any clue what was going on with her husband. He had just driven off without a word. I told her she'd better talk to HBS. And then I packed a few things and left. Turns out even though Grover's resolve was strong, his ability to express it was non-existent. He had simply grabbed his already-packed bag and driven off in his work van. No conversation, no note, no nothing. He just left. As he had predicted. We met up in a parking lot and just cried and cried. We held each other and cried. We had no idea what to do or where to go so we checked into a motel, drank a bottle of wine and began our new life together. We were scared, we were relieved, we were ecstatic and we were tortured.

Everyone around us was devastated. Our spouses, our kids, us, even our friends — devastated. There were gallons of tears on every front. Certainly more tears than Grover ever imagined. He had hidden his hunting rifle, fearing his wife would be so angry she would try to shoot him. But I knew better, mostly because I am a girl and I knew her. Kay wasn't going to shoot him. She was going to be devastated. And then try to make him stay.

In my camp, my husband was devastated but also mad. Mad enough to take down all my pictures (which he promptly put back up a few days later when he started trying to win me back). Funny how that works. You want what you can't have. Even if what you want is pathetic and painful. My poor distressed husband spent many sleepless nights researching relationships online, trying to figure out what went wrong. One morning when I arrived to pick up our son (whom I still ferried to and from school every day) HBS said, "I realize now what I did wrong and I hope one day you'll forgive me."

"Huh?" said I, totally confused. "What *you* did wrong?" Had he completely forgotten about all my lies and cheating and duplicitousness?

He replied soberly, "Yes. I realize now that all you ever wanted was for me to be emotionally available. And I was not."

Bingo.

"We can work on this," he pleaded. "We can go to therapy and fix our marriage. It's not too late."

I was washing the kitchen floor with tears. "Maybe," I sobbed, "But what about Grover? I am in love with him. What do I do with that?"

Aside from my sobbing, there was silence. He had no answer.

Weeks passed. Kay told me (on the phone) I was "despicable" and then refused to talk to me at all. My husband treated Grover with more kindness, telling me that he actually felt sorry for him. He said Grover was a pathetic man with no morals, seduced by the promise of frequent sex with little ole wanton me. He also told me that it would never work between Grover and me. We are too much alike, too volatile and too passionate, said he. He also ascertained that Grover was not the reason for my departure, merely the excuse. "You are leaving me because you have to," he stated firmly. "Not for Grover but for you. Which is why Grover will not last."

Smart boy, that ex-hubby of mine.

My mother, who adored my husband, also told me it would never work with Grover. "A relationship born of so much pain cannot survive," she said.

Through even more tears, I countered that Grover and I loved each other enough to endure all this pain.

"No, not your pain," she stated quietly. "The pain you have caused others. Your relationship will not survive that pain."

Damn, my mother was clever too.

We all soldiered on. The two ex-spouses spent more and more time together, calling in the middle of the night, nursing their wounds, comparing notes and crying together. I actually said to my husband one day, "You two should get together. All you have to do is get sexually attracted to one another and you'll be home-free. You've already done all the hard emotional work."

"That will never happen because it would be too convenient for you," he replied angrily.

Ha!

About five weeks after D-Day, Kay and I celebrated our mutual birthday. Yes, mutual. How crazy is that? Same day but I am two years older. My husband threw her a surprise party where a hundred of my ex-friends saluted her strength and courage, affirmed my heinousness, marvelled at her weight loss (she was on the trauma diet as well) and wiped away her tears of sorrow and gratitude.

Grover took me out for dinner, gushing at how wonderful it was to finally be able to do so openly, while I quietly brooded over the fact that I, the consummate party girl, no longer had very many friends. The birthday cards and calls were decidedly few that year.

Except from — of all people — my husband. On my actual birthday, he and Jack made me brunch and he gifted me a photo of the three of us taken years back on a ski holiday. We are a bedraggled bunch in that picture, me with no make-up and barely-combed hair, the two boys about the same (not that they ever wore make-up), but the smiles on our faces suggest a very happy time. I love that picture. He framed it next to some staggeringly appropriate Neil Young lyrics from the song *Already One*. He got it — we were already one. We had made a son and we were a family and nothing we could ever do was going to change that fact. Our little son would never allow us to forget, even if we wanted to. And our little son would always remind his daddy of his mama. Jack did (and still does) look a lot like me. Blonde, big blue eyes and a mischievous grin.

There were more waterworks that day, for sure. But more importantly, I was astounded by HBS's understanding. His resilience. His — dare I say — happiness? Even though it had only been five weeks since our split he seemed to be doing okay. Better than okay. This was no doubt due in rather large part to the next surprising and yet not completely unexpected turn of events. As fate would have it, in the midst of all the anguish, tears, begging, pleading and guilt, those two sadly beautiful and brutally betrayed spouses, Grover's and mine, fell in love. With each other. They found shared pain, then solace and finally love in each other's arms.

I was thrilled. All I ever wanted was for everyone to be happy. I reckoned this was a fabulous and fortuitous turn of events! I was already envisioning holiday dinners with all of us, kids included, around the merrily-festooned table, feeling love and gratitude and even a bit of mirth for the wacky way the world turns.

Yeah, right.

Grover completely freaked out. Because he had been replaced so quickly? Replaced by my husband? Or was it that his ex-wife, in spite of her new love, refused to let him off the hook even just a little? I don't think she found any of this wacky at all. She sure as heck wasn't planning Christmas dinner with me.

For some extra irony, no one was meant to know about this new development. According to Grover, who told me he got this information directly from his wife but I later learned may have gleaned it from reading her journal (the scoundrel!), she and her new lover were going to keep things clandestine for a year or so and then my ex was very sweetly going to ask permission from her daughters to date their mother. How darling. I could imagine that conversation taking place:

HBS: Hey girls, I've been sleeping with your mom for the past year. Would it be okay with you if I took her to the movies?

As if.

And yes, they most definitely were exploring carnal acquaintance. My ex is terrible at subterfuge and failed to hide the indisputable proof of their coitus on a day when he had asked me to come over to mind our sick son.

Oops. Those damned condom wrappers.

So the universe had a really good chuckle. I was the first to find out and Grover, naturally, the second. The new lovers begged us not to tell the children. Surely those poor kids had already suffered enough. Why cause them even more turmoil? Let them have some time to heal before introducing new complications.

Okaaaaaaaay.

To me it smacked more of high-horsedness (yes, I just made up that word). By this time, Grover and I were the pariahs of at least three counties. Our ex-partners were pitied and adored to the point of reverence. For the population of those three counties to suddenly discover that the spurned lovers weren't quite as decimated as initially presumed might inspire their thundering thud off those lily-white steeds. I can understand saving the kids from more upheaval. But isn't the truth the truth? And isn't withholding a BIG truth really just a lie? Shouldn't they too take their chances and honestly embrace the consequences of their choices and actions?

I thought they should.

However, guilt was still Grover's go-to emotion so he — and thus, we — agreed to keep our traps shut, at least for a while. His wife was just taking it one day at a time, she said. She had no idea where this new relationship was going. He never should have left her, she said. This never should have happened. Both marriages were good and should have gone the distance, she said. She and my ex were still in a state of shock. Who knew what might happen?

Well, there were a few clues. Like when HBS told me that if he could, he would scream his love for his new sweetheart from the top of a mountain. "Why can't you?" I asked. Seemed like a fine romantic gesture, one I know I most certainly would have enjoyed.

"Because of the children."

"The children? Oh, I get it. They are allowed to hate Grover and me for falling in love, just not you and yours."

"Vickie, don't you think you have done enough damage? For God's sake allow the children to have some peace."

It was a surreal carousel. Round and round we went. Kay to Grover, Grover to me, me to HBS, HBS to Kay, again and again. But a new narrative was beginning to emerge. I was getting the distinct impression from both HBS and Grover (Kay still would not speak with me) that I was the villain in this sordid tale of woe. Grover was just a feckless fool, naively seduced by my wantonly wicked ways. I was nothing more than the titillating temptress who had lured away a happily married man. Well who the hell was I to argue? All I knew was that I was hopelessly in love with Grover, he was all over the place emotionally, HBS and Kay "seemed" to be moving on, and all the kids (and many of our friends) hated me. Well that's not entirely true. Jack didn't hate me. He just didn't particularly respect me much.

Kay (via Grover) made it quite clear there would be no absolution for me — ever. Even my lovely ex-husband, the same man who had asked me to forgive him for being so emotionally unavailable during our union, hardened his heart towards me. The equation was obvious:

Me = bad.

Them = good.

Grover = stupid.

It was all pretty simple.

So there we were. Grover was all messed up, thinking maybe he should go back home, try to reconnect with his daughters, reunite with his wife and abandon me and our love in his quest for some semblance of redemption. My ex-husband didn't seem at all bothered by this, quite to the contrary in fact. He had no worries about his relationship with Kay and as for his feelings for me, I guess just desserts can be quite tasty. I have no idea what Kay was thinking (apart from what Grover told me). All I knew was that most days I was feeling very, very alone.

HBS and I had settled our financial affairs very quickly. In hindsight, we did it far too quickly, as I allowed my guilt to do my negotiating;

not a very wise move. After living in a downtown apartment for three months (with Grover, whose wife had no intention of vacating the barn), I purchased a townhouse at the edge of town as close as I could get to the old homesteads. I wanted Jack to be able to commute between his parents easily and at will. There was no way I could afford the old manse (HBS obviously could) and my sweet little abode was all mine. Sure, Grover lived there with me full-time for six months and yes he contributed as best he could but this was my nest. My haven. My retreat.

So there I was on a snowy February night, in that very townhouse, realizing it was most definitely time to cook something — for me!

You thought I'd never get back to the recipe, didn't you? Told you I might digress.

Artichoke-Asiago Pasta

I started with **1 can of artichokes. Drained and chopped**. I am in love after all (and artichokes never argue back).

I added about **8 garlic-stuffed olives**. Sliced fairly thin. I never even liked olives until I discovered these big beauties (probably in a martini). What an invention! Use them creatively and you'll never have to chop garlic again (such a messy sport).

Then what?

Well, how about some of that **spicy sausage** you know I love so much? It lasts forever and there's always some in my fridge. I went with 1/4 cup.

But I was craving more meat and I did have a plump **boneless chicken breast** in the fridge. I cut it up into bite-size morsels and fried it up. And I will tell you when I "fry" chicken I use my Teflon pan and absolutely nothing else. No oil, no butter — nothing. Just keep stirring and flipping and browning. It turns out great (and not greasy).

An old **celery stalk** in my fridge? Chopped up and in it went.

3 green onions, also chopped small. I added them.

I was really liking this process. I hate to waste food so I was cleaning out my fridge and inventing at the same time! If only cleaning up my love life could be this easy! Ah yes, my love life. Definitely in need of something — something outside the box. I mean face it — we were already way outside the box. I was in love with a man whose wife was involved in a relationship with my husband but, after a year of official separation, was back living with his ex-wife.

Oops. Forgot to mention that, didn't I.

See, after three months of apartment dwelling with me and six months of living with me in my new townhouse and eight months after learning about his wife's new relationship, Grover decided he had to go home. It was HIS family homestead after all. His business was there. His stuff was there. His kids were there (sometimes). His wife was there too (they had made no moves toward legal separation). He decided he had to compel his ex to either try again (he said she was sending signals) or leave (their home was owned by his father so her assuming permanent ownership was never in question). His guilt had reached epic proportions, his daughters were still barely speaking to him (and not to me at all) and because he needed to be at the old homestead every day for work, he felt he just needed to be there period. Staking his claim.

Leaving me and our relationship was collateral damage. Or so he thought. He left one frigid December evening only to return two nights later. It only took forty-eight hours for Grover to realize that our connection was huge and not easily dissolved. We were truly, madly in love. And Grover was truly lost. But as the weeks rolled by, he stuck with his plan. Kay's house became Grover's house again. Sort of.

See, the problem with his plan was Kay had no interest in vacating that home or giving up her new love. I reckoned her quest was more to get Grover away from me. Admit his mistake. Denounce our love. She told him that his relationship with his daughters would no doubt improve if he ditched me. She couldn't predict the future but leaving me certainly wouldn't hurt.

The monkey wrench here was Grover couldn't denounce our love because he still loved me. He just didn't know how to be with me with all this guilt crashing around. Not only his guilt over Kay but his guilt over his two daughters.

He moved back home. She had no legal ownership and therefore no choice. Did she relish this new arrangement? I have no idea. I doubt she was heartbroken that Grover was now officially away from me (even though we were still in daily contact). He slept on the couch. He tried to figure out things at home. He tried to stay away from me. Sometimes he succeeded, sometimes he did not. I was crazy with despair. The love of my life, the man of my dreams, the man for whom I had given up a huge part of my existence — that man was no longer with me.

But then again, he wasn't really with her either. He was just living there. And she was still hanging out regularly with HBS. It was all pretty messed up. I was pretty messed up too. Love and guilt are difficult bedmates. And you know what they say: *If they can do it with you, they can do it to you.* Grover may have promised me forever but hell, he had promised HER forever too.

Kay and Grover went to therapy. They talked and talked and talked some more. And every second night, when my son was with me, she slept with my ex-husband at his house. That ex, by the way, thought this whole new setup was dandy. He seriously had no problem with it whatsoever.

Does anything get any more outside the box?

So, on that particular night of creative cooking I decided that if I'm going outside of the box, I'm going big!

It came to me in a flash. So far I had artichokes (can the asiago be far behind?) and olives, meat morsels and green things. It all made sense. What would be surprising?

Mango. I decided to add fruit to this concoction. Why not? It may seem a little unorthodox but there's nothing wrong with fruit and meat together. I peeled and chopped the mango and tossed it in.

And since I was being wild and crazy I tossed in a **handful of cashews** too — what the heck!

Oh wait — what about **fresh baby spinach**? I added about a cup. I wouldn't even have to make a salad.

My large glass bowl (I use one of those oversized measuring cups, which I love because of the handle) was getting rather full. I gazed upon my creation and realized it needed pasta. Preferably **short pasta,** so it's easy to eat (no twirling required, what with all those chunky goodies). Luckily there was a box of bowties in my pantry. And of course, with pasta must come cheese. And with artichokes must come asiago. And there is always a gigantic wedge of asiago in my fridge.

I decided to be crazy yet again and added the **grated asiago (about 2/3 cup)** to the mix instead of sprinkling it on at the table, typical Italian style. I wanted it all melted into my medley.

But then: sauce? I needed some kind of liquid to bring this all together.

Well WTF, what about that jar of **homemade mango-citrus** dressing just sitting there on my counter, crying out to me? Why the heck not? It was there, it was ready and I wasn't making a salad, so why not? I dumped in about a cup. Unlike salad, I like a saucy pasta (I like a saucy man too). And then I stirred it all together, resisting the temptation to eat it right then and there, cause no matter how big that wooden spoon is I know I can fit it into my mouth and even cold this was looking darn good.

I boiled up the pasta according to the directions on the box. Always remember that if you like your pasta al dente — not mushy — you must taste, taste, taste and pull it off the heat while it is still a bit crunchy. Pasta will continue to cook even after you've dumped it out of the pot.

I put the whole big glass bowl of my favourite things (I should write a song for Julie Andrews: "Art-i-chokes on pasta and asiago with mango") in the microwave and cooked it on high for about 5 minutes.

The bowties (don't forget to drain them, silly) were in my huge pasta serving dish (you simply must get one of these!) and I dumped my spicy sweet cheesy artichokey sauce on top and mixed it all together. It looked and smelled magnificent!

Grover arrived for our date night. Yes, we still had them. When Jack was with his dad and Kay was at the barn, Grover came to me. It was all very orderly. Twisted but orderly. I didn't care. For me, ANY Grover was better than no Grover, and I took what I could get. I was so damned in love with him I probably would have traded ten years of my life for his love. His full-on, we'll-make-it-through-anything kind of love. You know the kind I mean?

Shortly before we left our spouses, but after conceding that it had to be done, during one of our secret encounters, Grover uttered those three special words. I responded, "I know, but do you love me enough?"

"Enough for what?" he asked.

"Enough to get us through all the pain that we are about to cause — and endure — and still love me?"

Turns out he didn't.

The crazy living arrangement went on for well over a year with no end in sight. Even after Grover realized that Kay didn't want him back and probably never would. She just wanted him away from me. So, they continued to share four walls. They shared sheets and towels and food and conversation. HBS told me he could see it lasting another five years, until our son was through high school. (Grover's daughters were both now out of the house.)

Huh?

He could see it, she could see it, Grover could see it, even my son was reasonably happy with it because it meant he didn't have to share his father with "the girlfriend" on a daily basis. And yes, the kids did find out, long before that first year was up. Probably because A) the exes spent an unusual amount of time together and kids aren't stupid and B) I'm very good at dropping hints.

Oops again.

Regardless, we all went about our merry business. I was becoming increasingly frustrated. Grover and I were spatting more and more. He was trying to be everything to everyone, and I was trying to convince myself daily that it was okay that my lover was still living with his wife. Until the day I saw Grover's underpants flapping in the breeze on the wash line right next to his wife's flapping underpants. Turns out she was still washing his clothes when she wasn't busy sleeping with my ex-husband.

I lost it. It wasn't the first time, but it was the biggest. Because at that moment even I, with that massive, full-on, once-in-a-lifetime love that I felt for Grover, knew this couldn't go on.

He had once said to me: "Vickie, you and I will have to break-up before I ask her to leave the house. Because I've already hurt her enough. And you are the cause of that hurt. So now I'd rather hurt you than her. But if you and I break-up and she doesn't take me back and I meet someone new, they won't put up with this. And then she will have to leave."

Golly. That's exactly what happened. Three days after the flapping panties, he called and dumped me. On the phone. He felt guilty about her and guilty about me and one of us had to go. We both bawled like babies during this call and then he said, "Short-term pain for long-term gain. I love you but this will never work. So now it ends. For good."

The *for good* part stemmed from the fact that he had already left me three other times. Once after nine months when he thought he should go home but ended up living with his mother, once a month later when he barged back into the matrimonial house and once three months after that, when he became totally convinced that Kay wanted to give their union another try. That time he stayed away for eight weeks until he finally realized that she had no intention of reigniting their marriage and giving up the new love she'd found a few miles down the road. He called me crying and bam! — together again.

What can I say? He was the love of my life.

That final year started optimistically, with new promises, new compromises and loads of love. I kept thinking *Finally, it's over. They are not going to get back together. Now she will move out.*

Nope. Nobody went anywhere. I started spending a bit of time in their home (when she wasn't there) although I refused to sleep there. The fact that they were sleeping in the same bed on alternate nights on the same sheets was completely unnerving to me. It was intimate. It was familial. It was wrong.

It didn't, however, stop me from pissing in a few corners just to stake my claim. Once when she was away on a trip with my husband, I actually cleaned out the fridge, top to bottom. It was a disaster and

Grover complained about it constantly. So, I fixed the problem. He was delighted. She was not.

We also left cryptic poems for each other on the fridge. I had once gifted them with fridge magnet poetry — you know, individual words on magnets that you can arrange any old which way — and we both built tremendous and devastating poems with great flourish. My little sonnets went something like "forgiveness beautiful like flowers in sunshine." Hers went more towards "despicable slut burn in hell."

Childish we most definitely were. One time when I came to pick up Grover for a gig (he played harmonica in my band) she was standing in the kitchen window. I offered a feeble wave. She replied with a scowl and her middle finger. Yep, real mature. I'll give her credit though. She called Grover a few minutes later and asked him to apologize to me. She knew she was being a dork and she also knew I would relay this story to Jack who would in turn relay it to his father who is a man with zero patience for childish behaviour — especially from adults!

Fun and games that were pretty much never-ending.

And then those damn panties flapped. It was the straw that broke the camel's back. I didn't *think* I could do all this crazy for another minute. But Grover *knew* he couldn't. So I got the boot. From the relationship. No, he did not boot me out of my own townhouse. He left me there to cry and moved back to his old homestead full-time.

A few months passed. I tried to be resolute. I tried to be accepting. Interestingly enough, on the evening of that fourth and final dumping, my new friend Cassandra, who is Métis, and her son came to do a "smudge" with Jack and me. She had lovingly collected the necessary wild ingredients. We placed them in a ceramic pot, fired them up and sat on the floor holding hands. Then, as per her instructions, we all took turns gathering the smoke in our hands and directing it to the part of our body needing help.

For me, obviously, it was my heart. So, I welcomed the smoke and I prayed. I didn't ask for Grover's love as I had so many times before. I didn't ask for his daughters' forgiveness or his wife's acceptance or for her to move out or for him to move back in with me. I said: *God please give me direction. Please show me the right way. Please guide me.*

A few hours later the phone rang and Grover and I were history.

Thanks, God.

I think.

Those subsequent months passed in a blur of tears, wine, more disappeared lbs., a move, more tears, more wine and my eventual foray into the online dating world.

Grover found a new girlfriend. (He did the online thing too, only apparently far more successfully than I.) And his wife finally got her own boot and moved in with my husband. Just as Grover had predicted.

However, on that fateful townhouse kitchen "out-of-the-box" night, after all my selfishly succulent experimentation, Grover told me my pasta was the best meal he had ever eaten.

Ever.

Obviously it wasn't enough to save that relationship but I can't count the number of times I have whipped this (or a variation thereof) up at the last minute, totally impressing new suitors and old friends alike. It's all stuff I have in my fridge or pantry regularly; people think you're a genius when it all comes out willy-nilly and transforms into this amazing repast.

Thank goodness for artichokes and asiago and mango-citrus dressing!

Something Fishy in Vancouver!

AS I APPROACH MY DOTAGE (MAYBE I'M ALREADY THERE?) I am trying to eat more healthy foods, watch my portion sizes, exercise regularly and get all Zen whenever possible. I do a big walk every morning, and I also try for a thirty-minute yoga practice a few times a week, which actually involves only about twenty minutes of poses and stretches and ten minutes (five at each end) of relaxation and meditation. Zen is good, right? Especially if you're a bit of a Type A nutcase.

Not you. Me.

For me, cooking is Zen. Like I said, sometimes it's therapy. Sometimes it's just "busy hands." It is sensual and relaxing and creative, all things we need daily. Cassandra says that watching me in action is like watching a cooking show on television. Except maybe a bit more personal — and comical! I do like to make people laugh.

A few years back when I first started that online dating thing for the second time — the first time being that period of the eight-week Grover hiatus during which I went on eight dates with eight different guys, none of whom were even vaguely interesting to me, and even though I made the effort and got all dolled up and even happily paid my half of the evening's tab as protocol dictates, I typically ended the night weeping in my bathtub missing Grover horribly, and I do apologize for this run-on sentence but sometimes it's the only way to get stuff out there — I finally met a nice guy named Charles. Soon to become Charlie (at least to me).

Charlie was (still is) drop-dead gorgeous, hilariously funny on the phone, smart, an accomplished yoga instructor and, as luck and geography would have it, living on the other side of the country. We emailed, shared countless photos, chatted online and talked on the phone for hours every day. In his first email, he called me "astonishingly beautiful" and for a word-girl like me that special commendation held a lot of currency.

When I say "hilariously funny" on the phone, I mean the guy could make me laugh daily, usually out of the blue. Much like cooking, I am typically the comedian so I thought it was pretty cool that this guy had me in stitches. Because the distance between us was so great we couldn't exactly meet up for a drink the moment we were ready so we just kept chatting and emailing and chatting some more. We often discussed what *would* happen when we finally met.

"Is there anything that worries you, Vickie? Or scares you? About finally getting together with me?"

I paused for a moment, gathering my thoughts, trying to figure out how I was going to say what I was going to say without hurting his feelings or totally derailing our future. You see, Charlie was a thoroughly modern *west coast dude*. Which means he was as in touch with his feminine side as anyone I'd ever met. Yet when I asked him why he took up yoga he replied (in his lilting voice), "I used to play all the big boy sports. You know, football, soccer, basketball. And I was always sore. So, I started reading about yoga, and honey, that sounded like a lifesaver to me. Pretty soon I was doing yoga all the time, and teaching yoga, and had no time for those big boy sports anymore!"

He did still play squash (and well too) and if you're familiar with the Grouse Grind in Vancouver (a hellish steep walk up the mountain), he also did that a few times a week. The guy was BUFF! He was also pretty vain and sent me loads and loads of photos. Some taken on the day and some golden oldies. One set included some nude yoga pose pictures that his ex-girlfriend had snapped. They were damn impressive. Except he Photoshopped out his penis. It was just a blur. I exclaimed on the phone, "No wonder you're single! You don't have a dick!" (To his credit, he laughed.) I continued, "Okay then, so did you blur out your manhood because it's so tiny you didn't want to frighten me?"

He laughed again (thank God). "No Vickie, I blurred out my manhood because I didn't want the photos to seem pornographic. I think they are more like art."

Well, that they were. And honestly, I wasn't that concerned with the size of his dick. I was a little more concerned with his voice. Like I said, it was somewhat lilting. To the point of sounding almost gay. You know, in the stereotypical (almost comic) way. And so I mentioned it to him.

"You're kidding, right?"

That was his only response. And when I didn't immediately answer, he hung up. I was astounded. And scared. And then the phone rang again.

"Hey baby, Chuck here." His voice was gruff and loud and deep and decidedly masculine. In a weird comedic way. "How ya doin today, sweetheart? Just checking in before I hop in my truck and hightail it to the gym to lift weights and stare at all them cute asses!"

I was crying, I was laughing so hard. Chuck? He was definitely not a Chuck. Charles or Charlie but no way Chuck. Not even Chuckie.

"Do you like me better now?" He was back to his normal voice.

Well damn, I liked that the guy could make me laugh. I liked that the guy didn't take himself too seriously. I liked that he was gorgeous and buff and I liked that he liked me. It had been almost six months since Grover, and I was lonely. And horny.

We finally devised a plan to meet — it was New Year's Eve 2006 and I was going to fly out to Vancouver for our first "date." I was excited and terrified at the same time.

Shortly after Grover and I split (for the final time) I moved into a new home. I had come to the realization that I would most likely never share the barn with him (would be kind of crowded in that bed with him, his ex-wife and me) and my sweet little townhouse was just a tad tiny for entertaining and music-making. It was also a condo with loads of stupid condo rules and I hate being told what to do by anyone. So, Jack and I moved to a brand new bungaloft a few blocks away. He was happy because he was still in the "hood" with all his new-found friends. I wasn't happy (more like morosely miserable) but moving, unpacking and decorating gave me something to focus on while I tried to mend my annihilated heart. And the new house gave me a clean slate. No HBS memories. No Grover memories. Just Jack, me and our orange cat.

The night before my fateful journey to British Columbia, Cassandra was at my kitchen counter waiting for dinner, offering support and wisdom, and just generally talking me through my nerves. She knew how scared I was. And as I scurried around my workspace, grabbing things from the pantry and fridge, she just kept talking quietly, lulling me into a blissful sense of security. Until I bent over to retrieve the spinach from the bottom shelf of my fridge. Without skipping a beat she said, "Wow, Vick, Charlie is gonna be in heaven cause you have a really great ass."

This is why Cassandra is such a good friend. And this is why cooking brings me such joy. It makes me feel fluid and competent and sexy.

So, let's talk about fish, because we all know how good it is for you and eating more of it will make you sexy! Really. I've never much liked fish that tastes like fish (go figure) and I sure as heck don't like my dinner staring back at me. I mean, why do they do that in fancy restaurants? Does anybody actually eat the head? The scales? The tail? Yuck. Get rid of it, I say. I've never eaten a chicken breast with the head attached. Why do I need to see Nemo's face gazing blankly at me, inspiring guilt after every bite?

I buy trout fillets, salmon, sole, tilapia or whitefish. No muss, no fuss, no head, no blank stares, just fish that tastes good (and not too fishy). Now I realize that if I was really health conscious I would grill that fish with lemon, add a salad and be done with it. I'm not that health conscious. I still want a yummy meal. Preferably with a few healthy components.

I also love the idea of stuffing a fish. Not to mount on the wall (ick!) but to eat. Mostly because I love stuffing and really, we only get it twice a year (Thanksgiving and Christmas) and that is simply not enough. I've had stuffed fish in restaurants and I've bought frozen stuffed fish but I've never quite sorted out how you successfully get the stuffing into the fish. Another messy sport and you already know how I feel about messy sports.

The other thing is, I do not make stuffing from scratch. Holy cow, did I ever botch a batch one Christmas when I way overdid the sage! Now I just buy it in a box. It is so darn good I'm afraid I just keep tasting and tasting, long after I know it is so darn good. On holidays, I make lots of extra because quite frankly after all my taste-testing I count myself lucky to have some left to put in the bird.

And that's the thing: big old turkeys are easy to stuff (even easier if you buy the new pre-stuffed kind). Fish? Not so easy. So I don't. I just put the stuffing *on* the fish. Because ultimately the flavours all blend together in the pan, in your mouth and in your tummy. Why stand on ceremony? In/on — whatever.

So, here's my easy-peasy non-stuffed stuffed trout — with two variations no less!

Mango-Citrus Stuffed Trout

---

1 large or 2 small trout fillets (or whatever fish you prefer)

1 box stuffing mix (you pick the brand and flavour. I prefer traditional sage)

2 clementines or peaches or nectarines or mango, cut into pieces

handful of spinach

handful of cashews

1/2 cup mango-citrus dressing

Place the trout in a shallow roasting pan (I like to use glass because it doesn't stick).

Make the stuffing according to the package directions and dump the whole lot onto the fish.

Add the spinach, the fruit and the nuts and saturate it all with the dressing. Cover with tin foil and bake at 350F for about 45 minutes. I absolutely cannot tolerate gelatinous fish so make sure it's cooked through.

The other variation:

Cranberry Stuffed Trout

This one was born after a huge turkey dinner. What do you do with leftover cranberry sauce? And stuffing for that matter (on the off chance there is some)? Well, I have several (upcoming) suggestions but why not trout 'em up? Just substitute the cranberry sauce for the mango-citrus dressing. In this application, you'll want to spread the sauce directly on the fish and then add the other ingredients.

Baked Rice

I like to serve fish with rice and here is my foolproof baked rice recipe, passed down to me by my mama. And when I say foolproof I mean it, because you really can't kill this sucker. I hate soggy, glumpy rice and if you under-bake this, just put it back in the oven. And if you over-bake it (which I've done many times because you know how sometimes you're cooking and then you get talking and drinking wine and forgetting that there's something in the oven?), it just becomes more like fried rice and that's a good thing too.

---

2 cups long grain rice I always buy Uncle Ben's. I've tried no-name and it just doesn't cut it

3.5 cups hot water I know the package says 2 to 1 but what the heck do they know and in my experience a little less liquid is better

1 large glob (a tablespoon?) butter or a splash of garlic olive oil

1 Tbsp. chicken bouillon You know — the powdery stuff (or a cube or two)

Mix it all together and bake it (covered in a casserole dish) for at least 45 minutes (same time as the fish?) at 350F. Longer if you get drunk. It's just not a problem. Add a salad or some steamed vegetables and voila — a beautiful meal. And nothing fishy about it. And if you're really not a fish-lover, try the above with chicken or pork tenderloin; they both work just as well!

So you probably want to know what happened with Charlie, right? I stayed for a week.

First night (New Year's Eve): "You are adorable. Happy New Year! Let's have sex!"

Second night: "Holy Crap, did we have sex last night after knowing each other for exactly two hours? Must have been all that champagne. Who are you again? Oh yeah. Let's have sex again."

Third night: "I'm going to invite some friends over to meet you. Do you feel like cooking that artichoke pasta thing you were telling me about?"

Now this roller coaster getting-to-know-you wasn't exactly easy (particularly for me) because Charlie's "condominimum" (his word) is 500 square feet — about the size of a small hotel suite. It was difficult to not be on top of each other, which wasn't the worst thing in the world because he is a darn fine-looking man, but still — it was his turf. There were many moments when I felt a little lost and a whole lot vulnerable.

Thankfully, with his full support, I found myself in the kitchen. Believe it or not I had actually transported a jar of mango-citrus dressing across the country because *ya just never know.*

What you should know is that Charlie is a bit of a yoga-superstar in Vancouver, and he is the one who introduced yoga to my world. (I am eternally grateful.) After all, when I met him online and then decided to meet him in person, I knew I'd have to attend one of his classes. Not understanding a downward dog (most of my old boyfriends?) was out of the question.

I reluctantly joined a gym (I am *so* not a gym person) just to take yoga classes for a few weeks before our fateful meeting. It was certainly an introduction. I learned some poses, pulled a few muscles, tried not to laugh when people farted in class (no — never moi!) and discovered I was a complete expert in that final relaxation. It just wasn't the "real deal." Charlie's class was the real deal.

So, these friends...he had met them through his yoga class. They were all stretched and slim and confident and, um, *west coast.* Just totally Birkenstock. I'm sure you can understand my trepidation. Meeting your cyber-boyfriend's friends in a tiny space while you cook them dinner is naturally just a bit stressful. But you know me and cooking — I was Zen.

Charlie lit the candles, played great music, and my food was a huge hit. As a matter of fact, it was such a huge hit I sent home doggie-bags (actually doggie Tupperwares) with all the guests. This made me feel like a million bucks. Which just goes to show — never underestimate the power of a home-cooked meal. Even if it's someone else's home on the Pacific coast.

Yes, it was a fun night. We ate, we danced, we laughed, we drank, they left, we had sex.

Fourth night: "Let's drive across a big mountain range in a blizzard to go visit my friends in Kamloops." These were my friends and I was thrilled that Charlie agreed to the road trip. It was at times arduous, at times spectacular, at times uncomfortable (all that aloneness together in a VW convertible) and at times just plain old fun. My pals were delighted to see us, and Charlie and our host struck up an animated conversation while our hostess and I did the kitchen thing.

We did not have sex that night. That night I dreamt that Charlie and our host were lovers. Like, gay lovers. Obviously, I still had some doubts. Not really sure why because the one place where Charlie and I really excelled was the bedroom.

Fifth night (back in Vancouver): "I have some other friends from Ontario who are now here in Vancouver. Can we invite them for dinner?" (I am always so much more myself in the kitchen and truth be told I still wasn't entirely comfortable with Charlie.)

They came, I made stuffed trout, we had fun.

Sixth day: Yoga class. Seventy people in a huge room worshipping Charlie. Me in the back corner lamely trying to keep up with the eighty-five-year-old granny next to me. I'll tell you my pride took a bit of a beating that morning. But I did get my mojo back on our final night. We went to Charlie's favourite local bistro, sat at the bar, ate steak frites and had a lovely time. Even the bartender said, "You two look pretty damn good in love. Let me take your picture."

And he did. Take our picture. And we did. Look good. But were we in love? I went back for two more visits that winter. I always cooked something and we always had compelling conversations and interesting adventures. But no. We never did fall in love. But (and I'm really not allowed to use that word because Charlie told me that a "but" negates everything that came before it so banish it from your vocabulary!) we did love. Charlie often said, "I'm loving you." When I finally asked what the difference was between that and "I love you" he replied in the brutally honest fashion that only he could get away with, "I'm not in love with you. But I do love you."

Charlie continually propelled me toward authenticity. He wanted me to live in the moment — the real, exactly-what-is-happening moment. Not the moment that I was fabricating in my head, or the moment I was expecting to happen or the moment that played out like a Disney movie. You see, that was my problem. I called myself a "Disney Girl" because like most women of my generation I grew up with Disney movies and fairy tale endings and that is exactly what I wanted and felt I deserved.

Ha!

Grover taught me better. And Charlie solidified the lesson. It was starting to sink in that just maybe I was not going to get "saved" by a man. Maybe Prince Charming did not exist? Maybe my Cinderella fantasy needed to be put to bed? Maybe I needed to save myself? Charlie helped me get on that path even though I'm pretty sure I fought it every step of the way.

I will be grateful to that boy forever. He kindled in me a new outlook on life and love, brought yoga to my world, and granted me the temporary use of that great body. For me, for then, that was more than enough.

Pizzas and Flatbreads

YOU ALREADY KNOW HOW I FEEL ABOUT PIZZA CRUSTS (OR AT LEAST MAKING THEM). I am a confirmed crust buyer and when I buy, I always try to buy the thin ones. I'm not big on a lot of dough (unless it's green). I prefer to taste what's on top. It's also another one of those calorie things. I'd rather have two pieces of thin than one of deep-dish/rising crust whatever.

Now being the trendy (ha!) girl that I am, I've recently become a big fan of flatbreads. Same idea, different shape and now readily available in any supermarket. These are a great dinner party staple. Do up a few different varieties, add a salad and you will have some very happy guests.

A few years ago, my friend and guru, Francis, was sitting at my kitchen counter and she watched me create this chicken/mushroom flatbread while she counselled me on life and love. When I say she is my guru, what I mean is we have sat many times at many different kitchen counters, and in her living room, at restaurants, on picnic tables or in hot tubs, talking about life and love. We find these conversations are best served with several bottles of wine (we like to start with white and then switch to red) and we also find that at times I am the student and she the teacher; other times, our roles are reversed.

To me, this is the definition of true friendship. Francis is always the person I go to when I'm in need of "big picture" advice. She is a woman of faith and spirit and also an inveterate searcher of souls. Never one to leap into the most convenient lifeboat, Fran will tread water furiously, sputtering, coughing and flailing, until she reaches the promised shore. I love that about her. She doesn't let me off the hook with easy platitudes either. She makes me dig deep and then deeper. Because, as I constantly say to my son, it's okay to make mistakes. Just don't make the same ones over and over again. Francis ensures that I learn the lesson and she never condemns me for making the mistake.

I also love that she loves to eat and she loves to cheat. She worked in the Toronto restaurant business for years so she knows a thing or two about good food. She makes a scrumptious curry with canned cream of chicken soup!

So, on this particularly jovial evening, we drank a tarty New Zealand Sauvignon Blanc, talked about my love life (or lack thereof) and she watched me build and bake a throw-together flatbread. We enjoyed every last crumb. The next day she emailed to say she was trying to remember all the steps because she had every intention of making it when she cooked for a friend in the near future. High praise indeed! And I love that she just wanted to cook something that is darn simple and darn good.

Chicken and Mushroom Flatbread

1 flatbread

cremini (or any kind of) mushrooms You'll have to decide what amount, depending on the size of your flatbread. And just so you know, I've actually used canned mushroom pieces on this and they're yummy!

dash Montreal steak spice

1 Tbsp. butter

2 Tbsp. pesto

1 large (or 2 small) boneless skinless chicken breasts

1 cup asiago cheese, grated

or

1 cup goat cheese

Sauté the mushrooms in butter, just like you did for the mushroom salad, adding the steak spice at the end. Now you may be wondering why I want you to sauté in butter as opposed to the far healthier olive oil option. I'll tell you why. Quite simply, it tastes better. I've tried olive oil (and grapeseed oil and cooking spray) with mushrooms and I just can't reproduce the flavour! There's something about butter and mushrooms together that is divine. Especially when you're caramelizing them at the end. Now, with that said I have recently discovered garlic olive oil, which I adore. So, if you can find it, use it.

Set the mushrooms aside and in the same pan fry up the chicken, which (of course) you've chopped into bite-size pieces just like you did for the artichoke pasta. Spread the pesto on the flatbread. Add the cooked chicken, mushrooms and then top with the grated asiago or the goat cheese (which you will have to either cut into thin slices or attempt to crumble - not always the easiest thing).

Bake at 400F directly on the oven rack (or on a pizza stone) for 10-12 minutes, until the crust is golden. Let sit for a few minutes and then serve...and eat!

Shayann's Triple Mushroom Pizza

You've already met my wonderful friend, Shayann, but what you don't know is that Shayann loves mushrooms. Mushrooms are her artichokes. She's definitely a shroom-aholic.

Shay lived close to me and was also a single mom (to two boys) so she and her brood would come for dinner at least once a week. It was actually quite a symbiotic relationship. She hates to cook but she loves to fix things. And paint walls. I love to cook and am entirely disinclined to hold a hammer or a paintbrush. So we would trade off on our skills. I actually called her my husband sometimes. You already know how much I loved to please my real husband at dinnertime, so when Shay came to dine, I felt kind of guilty if mushrooms didn't somehow factor into the culinary equation. That certainly led to some interesting creations and this is one of them — a simple variation on the above.

1 pizza crust or flatbread

1 cup cremini mushrooms, sliced thin

1 cup white mushrooms, sliced thin

1 Tbsp. butter

1 can sliced mushrooms, drained (no-name is fine)

3 Tbsp. pesto

1 Tbsp. Montreal steak spice

1/2 cup asiago or Parmesan, grated

You may have noticed by now that, much like artichokes and asiago, mushrooms and Montreal steak spice go hand in hand in my kitchen. I rarely sauté mushrooms without that kicky spice. But please feel free to experiment. If steak spice isn't your thing, find out what is. And if you're on a low-sodium diet, check out some of the new salt-free spice medleys.

In a large skillet, sauté the fresh mushrooms in butter or garlic oil. Any fresh mushrooms will do (portabellas, shiitake, oyster — go ahead and experiment). About halfway through the "fry" (you've done this enough times now — you're an expert) add the canned mushrooms. Then the steak spice (you know the drill). Spread the pesto on the crust, spoon out the mushroom medley, top with grated cheese. Bake this shroomy delight at 400F directly on the oven rack or your pizza stone for 10-12 minutes, until the crust is golden.

And if you're looking for a little variation, just do up the mushrooms and use a toasted baguette. Slice it the long way (like a Parisienne baguette sandwich), toast it first (in a toaster or under the broiler), top with pesto, mushrooms and cheese, and broil till the cheese is bubbly. Add a salad and you've got a fabulous lunch or casual dinner. And a very happy friend named Shayann.

Roasted Red Pepper and Goat Cheese Pizza

1 pizza crust or flatbread

1 large red pepper

1 cup pepper goat cheese

1/2 cup chives, chopped

1/2 cup Parmesan

I used to think roasting a red pepper must be an intricate, arduous task, known only to executive chefs and Italian mamas. It ain't.

On the barbecue: ready for this? Turn the barbecue on high, place the whole darn pepper on the grill and watch it burn. Keep turning so that all sides burn evenly. Yes — burn, baby, burn. The skin will turn black but that's okay because you're just going to scrape it off anyway.

If it's not barbecue season (and I know lots of winter barbecuers — I am just not one of them!), just put the pepper on your oven grill under the broiler. Same deal: keep turning until it is black all over. Remove the pepper from the heat and scrape/peel the skin off to reveal the lovely roasted veg beneath. Chop it into bite-size pieces.

Now here's another cheat and once again I must give credit to my ex-hubby's new wife (they're common-law now so I guess it's official): roasted red pepper spread. Back when she was still married to Grover, she served it up one evening with crackers. It was divine, and I asked for the recipe. She refused, laughingly. I begged. She still refused. I pleaded. She finally relented and secretively escorted me to her kitchen. And there it was, in her fridge. The jar of roasted red pepper spread that little Miss Cook-Everything-From-Scratch had purchased at the supermarket! We both laughed ourselves silly and I became an instant fan. So, if you don't feel like roasting a pepper, just use the spread!

I like to use the pepper goat cheese on this one because it provides all the spice you need — don't worry about adding anything else! Warm it up in the microwave until it's soft but not liquid.

Spread the cheese on the crust with a big spoon. Top with red pepper pieces or spread. Sprinkle with chives and top with Parmesan. I will admit that I love fresh Parmesan and I will also admit that it is so darn expensive I often settle for the stuff in a jar. Either way, it's all good.

As usual, bake at 400F directly on the oven rack for 10-12 minutes, until the crust is golden. Let sit for a few minutes, serve and eat!

I do like simple pizzas, not overloaded, not too many ingredients, not too many things to fall onto the floor before they reach your mouth. But if I was cooking for Shayann, I would add portabellas to this one. Cut them into long slices, fry them up in butter and steak spice and add them to the mix. Delish!

Garlic Mashed Potato Pizza

What, you say? Mashed potatoes on a pizza? Are you nuts? That's what most people think. Until they eat it. Then they just want more.

I discovered this one at a restaurant celebrating garlic days. It sounded so crazy and intriguing I had to try it. Once I tried it I had to try to make it. Once I made it I had to eat it, which is the biggest trouble with this pizza: so addictive. Especially if you like comfort food. And also when you cheat — easy-peasy.

1 pizza crust or flatbread

1 package boxed garlic mashed potatoes (what — you thought we'd make them from scratch?)

1 cup of precooked bacon, chopped

or

1 cup of spicy Italian sausage, chopped into tiny morsels

or

half and half — depending on how much kick you want

1 cup Parmesan cheese

1/2 cup chopped chives

Cook the mashed potatoes according to the directions on the package. Spread the potatoes on the crust and top with bacon and/or sausage and chives. Top that with Parmesan and bake at 400F directly on the oven rack for 10-12 minutes, until the crust is golden.

You might want to make two. Seriously. It also makes a superb breakfast!

Jack's Honeybean Pizza

Okay, first of all, there is no such thing as a honeybean. We're actually using maple baked beans here. It's just that when I started making this pizza, Jack was about eight and for some reason he called them honeybeans. It stuck. Kinda like "ronis" — boxed macaroni and cheese — "ronis" as in macaRONIS. I have no idea how this stuff happens, it just does. Same with honeybeans which, by the way, he also absolutely loves on tacos. Or just topped with melted orange cheddar. Believe it or not, at the ripe old age of nineteen, he was still calling them honeybeans. He's twenty-seven now and has finally learned the real name, but for me this will always be Honeybean Pizza.

1 pizza crust (you may want a thicker one for this because it gets a little heavy)

1 can maple brown beans (no-name is fine)

1 large tomato, diced

1 green pepper, chopped

1 cup mozzarella, grated

Spread a thin layer of maple beans on the pizza crust. Add the tomatoes and green pepper and top with grated cheese. Bake at 400F directly on the oven rack for 10-12 minutes, until the crust is golden. Broil for about a minute just to get the mozzarella bubbly and a tiny bit brown. Honestly, kids really love this pizza. Must be the honeybeans.

Breakfast Pizza (aka The Perfect Hangover Breakfast)

Not that I've ever been hung over. Well, why the heck wouldn't you eat breakfast pizza? You've eaten cold pizza for breakfast, right? Why not actually make one especially for the occasion?

1 pizza crust (or large flatbread)

4 eggs, scrambled

bacon or ham, chopped

1 Tbsp. olive oil (or pesto if you're feeling frisky)

whole bunch fresh ground pepper

1 cup cheese (your choice), grated

Optional: diced tomatoes, green peppers, green onions, mushrooms

Scramble up those eggs and cook the bacon (nice and crispy would be my choice). Better yet, buy the bacon that is already precooked and just chop it up. If you prefer ham, chop that up. Spicy sausage (you're a huge fan now, right?) — go ahead. Really, whatever meat you like will do. If you're a vegetarian, no meat. Whatever!

Spread the oil or pesto on the crust, top with the scrambled eggs, add the meat and pepper and any of the optional ingredients you may choose and top with your favourite grated cheese. Bake at 400 F directly on the oven rack for 10-12 minutes, until the crust is golden.

The beauty of this little breakfast treat is that you can make it the night before and simply refrigerate until you are ready for baking the next day. Absolutely perfect for a hung over morning, don't you think? I mean, that's what I've heard...

My Jewish Phase

AND THEN THERE WAS BEN. Well, to be honest first there was Noah and then there was Ben. I call this my "Jewish Phase." After Charlie and I parted romantic company I headed west one more time in pursuit of l'amour. I was so in love with Vancouver I was determined to move there one day, so I figured I might as well look for love in western regions. About three months later I found Noah online. He was very smart, very witty, a wonderful writer and lovely to look at. Not in the model-gorgeous way that Charlie was, but in an interesting European-scholar way. Because Noah is actually Russian. A Russian Jew, to be more precise. A Russian vegetarian Jew with a very strong Russian accent.

This made for a somewhat comical first phone call.

"Hello Wickie? Wickie, ees zat you? Eet's Noah here, so wary happy to talk wiss you finally my dear Wickie!"

I wasn't prepared for the accent and I kept bursting into fits of laughter every time he tried to speak. Honestly, I felt like I was chatting with a cartoon character. Thankfully, Noah has a wonderful sense of humour and was willing to forgive my rudeness. We made plans for my western sojourn and off I flew. There were several provisos because I had (believe it or not) learned something from my previous experience.

#1. I would stay in a hotel. Even though Noah assured me that his loft was quite spacious and I could have the bedroom and he would take the sofa, I stuck to my guns. 24/7 on a first "date" is just plain stupid. Trust me.

#2. We would explore friendship before lust.

#3. We would split the cost of my flight 50/50. I was prepared to foot the bill for my hotel room.

Everything went swimmingly. On my first evening Noah introduced me to his fabulous Labradoodle, Moby, the ultimate inspiration for Shiloh, my golden doodle. We ordered Indian food, something new for me. I loved the dog and I loved the cuisine, even without meat. I was determined to master some cheater recipes upon my return home. I loved hanging out with Noah, talking, walking the city (alone and with him and Moby), visiting his friends and enjoying summertime in Vancouver. Alas, I did not fall in love with Noah (or he with me). But I did not regret the trip for a moment.

Oops. I just said "but." Which reminds me that on my final day Charlie actually picked me up to share lunch and a drive to the airport (Noah was working). We had a great time together without the pressure of romance and actually shared not only lunch but a huge juicy kiss at the airport!

As I sat in the terminal waiting for my flight, I was sipping a glass of wine and smiling about the weekend's outcome when my cell phone rang. It was Ben.

Ben was another online connection I had made just before departing for the west. His photo kept popping up on the dating website in that scrolling header that is intended to pique our curiosity and compel us to action. He had dark hair and a dark mustache and looked a lot like my Grade 12 boyfriend. So I emailed him: "You look a lot like my Grade 12 boyfriend."

He replied instantly: "Don't you remember? I was your Grade 12 boyfriend!"

That cracked me up because there is no way Ben was my Grade 12 boyfriend because:

1. His profile said he was six years younger than I am and my Grade 12 boyfriend was five years older. Now when I say his profile *said*, it's because if you online date for any length of time you learn that at least half the participants are lying about

their age. At that time even I, "Miss Newfound Honesty," was lying about mine (I think I had shaved off three years).
2. Ben lived in Thornhill, a community north of Toronto that had never really figured into my life whatsoever.
3. Ben was Jewish, and I had never dated a Jew. Well, until Noah, and I wouldn't exactly call that a date. And Noah was much more a Buddhist than a Jew.

One of my girlfriends had dated and lived with a Jew. She was madly in love with him, and he seemed totally smitten with her. Until it was time to get married. Then he married a fellow Jew. She got dumped and depressed and he married a Jew because he had to.

So the first time Ben and I chatted online I came right out and said, "Shouldn't you be with a Jew?"

"You must know some Jewish people," he said.

And then a few moments later, when I realized I actually liked him and asked if I could call him on the phone he said, "I dunno...can you call a Jew?"

So you see, Ben is a funny guy. And I like funny.

Noah was funny too. The not so funny difference between Noah and Ben is that Noah is a very spiritual guy of Jewish lineage but not a practicing Jew. Ben is a seriously practicing Orthodox Jew who keeps kosher and, as I learned on our first date (he took me to his favourite restaurant in Toronto), living with celiac disease. This means he must adhere to a gluten-free diet. No bread, no pasta, no pizza. Put together kosher and gluten-free at a regular Toronto bistro and you've got a date with a guy who can't have meat, poultry, seafood, bread, pizza or pasta.

That left salmon. And vegetables. Ben could have salmon and vegetables.

And Ben hates salmon.

Anyway, yes...Ben and I chatted as I prepared to depart Vancouver, made plans for our initial date, and the long and the short of it is we had fun in spite of his dietary limitations. So I invited him to dinner. I am a chef after all, and a few little culinary hurdles were not going to stop me from working my magic.

Ha!

That's when I learned the other thing about Ben. He needs gluten-free and he needs kosher but he is also (and I say this with the utmost affection) the pickiest eater who ever set foot not only in my kitchen but on this planet! The pickiest!

He wanted spaghetti. His way.

The rules: No chunks. No chunks of tomatoes. No sireee, you sure wouldn't want any chunks of tomato in a tomato-based sauce.

Mushrooms. Those chunks are allowed. But they have to be from a can.

Corn pasta only. Not rice pasta. Rice pasta is too glumpy. Fair enough, but do you know how hard it was to find corn pasta back in 2007?

A rosé sauce would be his preference. That's what he told me on the phone. He would prefer a rosé sauce. Cheeky little celiac Jew, don't you think?

Thus was born **Ben's Spaghetti,** and I'm going to tell you right here that I am embarrassed by this one.

Ben's Spaghetti

---

1 jar basic tomato spaghetti sauce Just check the label for wheat or gluten

1 jar basic cream pasta sauce Or even, my goodness, a Rosé sauce. Again, check the label

1 can mushroom pieces (he doesn't like the whole ones), drained

Spices (garlic, basil, oregano) to taste

Salt and pepper

Parmesan, grated

Corn pasta (I used spaghetti but it comes in several shapes and sizes)

Dump all the ingredients into a pot and heat 'em up. Cook the pasta according to the package directions. Strain and serve with sauce, topped with Parmesan. Serve with a semi-Caesar salad and by "semi" I mean romaine and dressing only, obviously no bacon or croutons. Enjoy the heartfelt accolades from one very happy celiac Jew who thinks you have somehow worked a miracle. Like I said...embarrassed.

I actually did try to be more inventive for Ben. One night I whipped up a trout/vegetable medley using my mango-citrus dressing over corn penne. He wouldn't even touch it. Not a big fan of trout and too many chunks. Funny how vegetables come in chunks that way.

For his 50th birthday celebration — and this is where the hilarity really kicks in because it turns out Ben had shaved a full five years off his age (the little liar) and we are really only two years apart — I asked him to bring along some kosher steak (no kosher butchers where I live) so we could have fondue. He was reluctant because it's not just about the meat. The utensils have to be different. This means dairy spoons can never touch meat knives, so pots and cutlery and every damn thing you use to cook with has to be kept separate. At his house he has two separate drawers. So the pot in which we were going to cook the beef could never have seen any dairy. Ever.

Well, I do like a nice cheese fondue so damn, my existing pot wasn't going to cut it. I went out and bought a brand new one (I wanted one anyway...no, really) and new forks and knives too. Then I checked the label on the can of consommé, which is what I like to simmer the small cubes of steak in. Gluten! There is actually gluten in consommé! So I rushed over to the gluten-free aisle and lo and behold found gluten-free beef broth. Thank you, God! I bought little canned potatoes (they're awesome in the broth and only take a moment) and canned whole mushrooms (I prefer fresh but I already know Ben) and made the semi-Caesar salad and even bruschetta on gluten-free crackers. I baked the birthday pie (see recipe below), lit about thirty candles and put on my new blue dress and high heels and soft music — and damn! — I was ready to celebrate that boy's birthday!

The one thing I invented for Ben (who has quite a sweet tooth) that doesn't embarrass me is this gluten-free chocolate cream pie.

Remember I talked about the easy-peasy shortbread pie crust? The regular version is coming right up, but here is the gluten-free rendition.

Gluten-Free Chocolate Cream Pie

1/2 cup very soft butter

1/3 cup white sugar

1/4 tsp. vanilla Make sure it's pure. If it's not it will contain gluten!

1 cup rice flour

1 package cooked chocolate pudding

1 small carton 35% whipping cream

1/4 cup sugar

chocolate shavings

For the crust: cream the butter (nuke it first if you have to), sugar and vanilla. Blend in the flour. Spread the dough on the bottom of a pie plate. Now here's the funny thing: when I make this with regular flour and use a glass pie plate, it serves up quite nicely. But when I tried it for the first time with rice flour it really stuck to the bottom. So I switched to a tin pie plate (mostly so that Ben could take the leftovers home) and then it served up beautifully. I have no idea why.

Bake at 400F for about 20 minutes — until the crust is a toasty brown colour.

Cook the pudding as directed on the package. You know when they say "stir constantly"? STIR FUCKING CONSTANTLY! I tend to be a bit of a multitasker in the kitchen and if you don't stir constantly you're gonna end up with burnt pudding and a burnt saucepan. This I know from experience. So stir constantly!

Let the pudding cool slightly but not long enough to form that yucky film on top, and then pour into the baked pie shell. Allow this to cool thoroughly before topping. When I say thoroughly I do mean thoroughly because one time I was in a hurry and I didn't and when

I dolloped the whipped cream onto the pie it completely melted into the hot filling. Let it set!

Whipped topping: Beat the whipping cream on high until it's all fluffy and peaky, gradually adding the sugar as you go. Again, the sugar is to taste. If that was up to Ben it would be a barrel-full but I reckon there's already enough sugar in the crust and the filling so 1/4 cup should do it. Dollop it onto the pie and top with your favourite chocolate, shaved from a bar. I just use a paring knife and literally whittle away but you could use a grater too. You don't need a lot — it just looks pretty.

So, back to dinner. The funny (not) thing about the fondue was Ben wouldn't touch the gluten-free beef broth because the beef in it wasn't kosher. Doh! So I ended up sautéing the steak, potatoes and mushrooms in oil and spices and we ate it with my new kosher cutlery, salad on the side. And here's what's really funny. A few months later I checked the label on the gluten-free beef broth and there's actually no beef in it at all. Just beef flavour. So he could have had it! Doh again.

He did go absolutely crazy over the pie. I'm pretty sure if I'd turned Jewish and kept on making it he would have married me. Okay, maybe not, but we have remained "friends for life." You see, during our first phone call Ben said, "Vick, you gotta know one thing about me. Once I make a friend we are friends for life. Got it? No ifs, ands or buts. A friend is a friend is a friend. Forever." *Yeah sure*, thought I. Famous last words from a guy who obviously hasn't done the online dating thing as much as I have. I had enjoyed several dates (and I mean *enjoyed*) but had no interest in pursuing anything romantic with the guy. But I was always open to friendship. Turns out not ONE of those guys felt the same. If I didn't want love (or at the very least sex) I was getting nothing, damnit.

Oh the torture.

I'm kidding. Bu-bye.

With Ben the rules were different from the get-go. He knew we could never "mate." He knew that I knew that we could never "mate." We could date and have dinner and go to concerts and have sex but he would never be my boyfriend (officially) and we would certainly never marry (not that I wanted to). He knew that I fully understood the Jew thing. Ben was always straight-up with me about who and what we were (even when he told me I was a better Jew than most Jews he knew). Funny how there are times when all the honesty in the world doesn't stop your heart from dreaming. Why do you think they call us "hopeless" romantics?

Yes, there were moments that I went all Disney wishing we could go the distance. Hard to believe, I know, especially after all of those big fat Charlie lessons. I guess it takes some time (and effort) to truly banish that Disney girl. I also guess you have to really WANT to truly banish that Disney girl and I'm not sure I was there yet. But the truth is I kind of doubt Ben and I would have gone the distance even without the Jew thing. We had some other pretty fundamental differences, and we scrapped a lot. We're both stubborn as hell and when we argued, no one gave an inch.

What we did do well was a lot of laughing. We both derived a certain amount of glee from toying with each other — in a fun way. Case in point:

"Hey Ben, you know what?"

"What Vick?" (He always called me Vick.)

"I love you."

"Oh geez, come on Vick..."

"No seriously Ben, I really do love you. You know, like real, honest, simple love — no expectations, no commitments — just pure, joyful love. That is how I love you. Not I "*love* you" now you must commit to "*love* me". I just love you no matter what the outcome is. Or is not."

Ben: audible sigh of relief.

"So tell me something," I continued, realizing that he wasn't going to say anything. "Now that you understand this new definition of love, do you love me?"

Ben: more nervous laughter and another "Oh geez, come on Vick..."

He didn't say it but I figured he loved me enough to spend Christmas morning with me — on the phone. In those days I was alone Christmas mornings because Kay's family is German so their big celebration is Christmas Eve. HBS's family is spread around the world so her Christmas would be his Christmas, much like my family's Christmas had been his Christmas. Jack was reluctant to leave me alone on this hallowed night (he knew it was my favourite night of the year) but I insisted he go with his dad. So yes, I was alone until whatever time my son showed up with his dad (who would stay for gifts and brunch) on Christmas morning.

Actually there was one Christmas morning that Jack and Grover were with me. It was the only Christmas that Grover and I spent together without drama (six months before he dumped me that final time). Jack had asked to be dropped at my place after his Eve celebrations because I was "way more fun on Christmas morning than Dad and Kay" (who liked to sleep in). That was a special Christmas for me.

But on this particular one (two years later) I was alone Christmas morning. And for an Orthodox Jew, Christmas is just another day off so I made coffee, called Ben and we chatted for two hours. It was lovely.

He also liked to play guitar and sing (and was damn good at both) and we often jammed. Sometimes I'd play piano and he'd sing, sometimes he'd play guitar and I'd sing and we even wrote a song together.

We were apart on New Year's Eve that year. I had a gig and he had his friends in Toronto; a large posse I had never met. At that point in our relationship I knew where Ben and I were going (nowhere), so I had invited another new prospect to be my New Year's date. This could have been all nice and fine (the new guy was highly smitten with me and I was willing to explore) except Ben and I had, completely unexpectedly, spent the night before together. In previous months we had spent a few nights together at his place because I do not drink and drive. The first was after my office Christmas party (he was my date). We lay in bed for hours — and I mean literally hours — listening to his vast collection of R&B. Ben and I have very similar tastes in music so every new song inspired an "Oh, I love this one" or an "Oh, I haven't heard this one in years!" It really was a magical night. But Ben doesn't drink much so when he visited me in Guelph he always went home. The boy liked to sleep alone (no touching, thank you kindly) and I think it was also his way of setting boundaries. Reminding me of the rules. The "you can 'love' me rule; just don't fall in love with me."

But on that night before New Year's Eve, he had come to my regular gig (first and only time!) and for whatever reason opted to come home with me. To my house. And stay the night. Was it New Year's guilt? A belated Christmas offering? I didn't care. It was wonderful. In the morning, he even fried me eggs the way his mama had taught him. It was so damn hard to say goodbye and hard to watch him go that morning. I was definitely going Disney. Needless to say, as I sang my heart out that evening, my head was full of Ben. The poor other guy didn't stand a chance.

Shortly before midnight I sent Ben a text: *If I could choose one person to kiss at midnight, I would choose you. Happy New Year, Ben!*

I got his reply immediately: *Happy New Year, Sweetie. I love you.*

And you wonder why I go Disney?

Still, not all stories have fairy tale endings (are there any Jewish fairy tales?) and I'm just happy that Ben came into my life. The official dissolution of our relationship was a tear-fest (for me) and a manly demonstration of resolve (for him).

"Come on Vick...you know you are getting in too deep. You know I can't take you where you want to go. You've always known."

Me: snivel.

Ben: "Damnit Vick, I don't think we can do this anymore."

Me: snivel louder.

Ben: "I thought you knew this was just going to be light. You know, fun."

Me: snivel louder, then sob.

Ben: "Okay Vick, honest, I gotta go. I'll call you tomorrow, okay but I really don't think we should see each other anymore. At least not for a while. You gotta get your head back on straight."

Yes, indeed I did.

I sobbed buckets after he left. My brain knew everything was unfolding as it must. My heart felt clobbered. Not annihilated, just beat up. And it was pretty much my own damn fault. So I pulled myself together and wrote him a heartfelt email, thanking him for all the amazing moments we had shared. It sucked that there would be no more, but I knew he was right.

The epilogue: three months after we "broke up" and I had moved on to my next relationship, I visited Ben who had just undergone surgery and was somewhat immobile. It was around his birthday and I brought lunch and, of course, pie. This was our first encounter since that tearful farewell night and it was really nice. We had a wonderful chat during which I told him all about my new boyfriend. I think he was surprised but at the same time genuinely happy for me. When I went to leave he gave me the absolute biggest, warmest hug he had ever offered and asked me to come back again soon. And then he said, "I love you." It still ranks way up there as one of the best "I love yous" of my life. And that's why I'll happily bake that chocolate cream pie for him anytime he wants.

Easy-Peasy-Lemon-Squeezy Pie

So if you're not gluten-free, try this!

---

1 shortbread crust (as above except use regular flour)

1 package lemon pie filling

Big squirt of lemon juice

2 eggs

1/4 cup sugar

I make this one for my gluten-ous friends and it's always a big hit. Even though you're cheating like crazy with the boxed filling, everyone thinks you made the whole darn thing from scratch because of that shortbread crust!

Make the crust exactly as above except use regular flour (unless you're cooking for Ben and goodness knows he could use a new girlfriend). Make the filling as per the directions on the package except add that squirt of juice for extra zing and top with meringue (also as per the package). This is so easy-peasy and obviously lemony-squeezy and trust me — it's all about the crust!

Currying Flavour

THIS ONE IS SO DEAD SIMPLE, MUCH LIKE BEN'S SPAGHETTI, I'M ALMOST EMBARRASSED TO INCLUDE IT IN THIS BOOK. But remember how I said I wanted to develop some cheater Indian food after Noah? Well, it turns out I have a few curry-loving friends and this is super easy and always a big hit. Speaking of easy, I recently cooked this for my friend, Lisa. Now Lisa is probably only easy with her fabulous husband, Stephen (and who wouldn't be?), but she is notoriously un-easy in a few other areas of her life. And rightly so. Lisa owns and operates a very successful company and that is not a life for sissies. She is used to getting things done and getting them done her way. Can you spell "Bitch on Wheels"?

Case in point: I once invited all my girlfriends to a photo shoot because I wanted to have wacky black and white pictures of my wacky girlfriends and me in my new black and white powder room. There was some wine involved (is there ever not?) and we did get wacky because I refused to let any of these girls "pose." It was all about fun. Well, except for Lisa. Fun or no fun, no one tells Lisa what to do. Ever. Not even me. So when she refused to get wacky for the camera, I politely asked, "What do you want to do?" And she replied in all seriousness, "I want people to look at our picture and wonder if we're lesbians."

Okaaaaaaaaaay.

I can assure you (and Stephen, who once said that if we were lesbians he wants to be one too) that we are not. But that one photograph has a certain sultry flavour to it, much like this curry that Lisa loves.

I'll also tell you here that she is not the easiest person to please on the culinary front. Once again, she makes no bones about what she likes, doesn't like or will refuse to eat. I once hosted a summer barbecue for a lot of friends and the only meat being grilled that day was beef (of the ground variety). Lisa informed me icily that she had not eaten a hamburger in twenty years! Thank goodness for salads and frozen shrimp.

Lisa and I are terrific friends and I love her to pieces, but I'm sure you can appreciate my trepidation. This woman has eaten in some of the finest restaurants in the world! The prospect of another hamburger debacle was only a little daunting.

Thankfully, she loved this curry. And I most certainly felt no compulsion whatsoever to share my cheats with her. But I will with you.

Chicken Curry with Baked Rice

So here's the trick to this super-easy dish: use cans and jars of curry sauce. Just find the ones you like. This may require many hours of taste-testing and what's not to like about that? Here's the other trick — the one that will fool your curry-lovers into thinking you just might be cooking from scratch: use two different cans/jars. Sometimes I use curry sauce and tikka masala. Sometimes curry and butter chicken. Sometimes two different curries. The wonderful thing about most supermarkets these days is they have amazing ethnic food aisles. Do not be afraid to experiment with everything and anything!

---

1 can curry cooking sauce

1 jar tikka masala

2 skinless chicken breasts, chopped into bite-size morsels

3 large carrots, peeled and chopped into bite-size morsels

1 large Vidalia onion, chopped into bite-size morsels

Rice baked just the way I taught you!

Brown the chicken in a large saucepan. Dump in all the canned or jarred sauces, whatever you decide to try. Add the carrots and onions. Simmer for as long as possible. Serve over that easy-peasy baked rice you have now fully perfected.

The last time Lisa and I had this, I actually used second-day curry (no doubt made for some boy the night before) and she couldn't rave about it enough. She even took some home for next day's lunch (yes, I always make a cauldron). It also freezes beautifully and nukes up for a quick dinner. If there's no rice, try it with some naan bread for dipping. Whether it's first-day or leftovers, serve it with a fruity mango salad, which will offset the kick from the curry. I like to eat my salad European-style: after the main course on the same plate. The curry remnants and salad mix together beautifully!

And then there is red curry. Remember my friend Francis, my guru? We had lunch at a Thai place once and she ordered red curry. At that time I was such a yellow curry cook I wasn't sure what to expect. Oh, how I loved her lunch! And I VIVDLY remember her saying to the waiter, "Please, hold the green peppers. Just lots of broccoli." Such a wise decision. Because if you're advancing in age like I am, you may also have learned that all those healthy veggies that you once adored (peppers, cabbage, leeks) no longer adore you. Especially the next day.

Anyway, I soon tried to duplicate this new red repast. I bought red curry paste and coconut milk and all the other ingredients and cooked my little heart out and it was okay. Probably too kicky (too much paste?) but okay. Not great. Just okay. Then I went back to the supermarket and lo and behold, what did I discover but a jar of red curry sauce. Yep. Just like the yellow stuff, red comes in jars all premade and everything.

Doh.

Now the thing that I really love about this curry is the bok choy. Much like spinach and artichokes, I've become obsessed with bok choy. And it is SO good for you.

Red Curry and Veg

> **2 jars red curry sauce** I make a big pot because I love leftovers
>
> **1 large head bok choy,** chopped
>
> **1 large stock broccoli,** chopped (or use frozen if you prefer)
>
> **3 green onions,** chopped
>
> **Optional: shrimp or chicken,** precooked
>
> And if you want even more veg, you could add **peppers (any colour), carrots or mushrooms**.

I'm sure you know the drill. Just mix it all together, simmer (but not too long if you want the bok choy a little crunchy, which I do) and serve over rice.

Turkey Curry Soup

As I mentioned earlier, I hate to waste food. My fabulous ex-hubby was not a big fan of day-old dinner unless it was spaghetti sauce. Grover, on the other hand, refused to waste a single morsel of anything, even if it was a touch brown, wilted, smelly and blue with mold. I choose to land somewhere in the middle. Funny, that. Maybe somewhere in the middle is always the place to land, even romantically?

After Grover and I gave up the final ghost, my ever-so-astute then thirteen-year-old son said, "Mom, I think you need to find a guy who is a cross between Dad and Grover."

Kids. They do say the darnedest things.

Anyway, I don't cook with anything that might be mistaken for penicillin, but I do love soup so, where there's a bone — leftover chicken, vegetables, potatoes (just about anything but salad) — there shall always be soup! And where there's turkey, there will be turkey-curry soup. Here's what you do:

After your big dinner, **remove as much meat as you can from old Tom's carcass, place it in a gargantuan stock pot, cover it with** water, add some salt, a few bay leaves and a splash of red wine and boil the crap out of that sucker for as long as possible. I mean, I'm not talking weeks here, but I've been known to let it go for twenty-four hours. After the crap has been boiled out, let it cool completely, wash your hands well and dig in to remove the bones. I know this may sound gross but trust me, it's the easiest way. I tried being all prim and proper (once) and used tongs and spoons and forks and it takes forever and doesn't do nearly as good a job. So just dig right in there and get those bones out!

Now that you're left with broth and bits of chicken, add whatever vegetables were left over from your festive feast. Add the mashed potatoes too — they'll just make your soup creamier and yummier. I've never actually tossed in leftover stuffing (probably because there never is any leftover stuffing) but I suppose you could even try that. I'd probably leave out the cranberry sauce. No pumpkin pie either. But just about anything else goes. Add a whole bunch of fresh ground pepper and simmer some more and then — whenever you feel like it — dump in a can of curry sauce. The same kind of canned curry sauce you used for the chicken curry.

And there you have it: Turkey-Curry Soup. Virtually almost-but-not-quite made from scratch!

Turkey Shepherd's Pie

This is another après holiday favourite in my home regardless of the fact that virtually everybody laughs about the concept before they taste it. Just ask Janice and Dale, that very same Vancouver couple who joined Charlie and me for stuffed trout. I invited them for a festive post-Christmas dinner (they had moved back to Ontario) and the very mention of turkey shepherd's pie sent them into fits of hysterics. Dale is British and I'm sure the very thought of bastardizing a colonial staple was ludicrous. Janice has known me a long time and just thinks I'm a nut anyway. So sure, I let them laugh. Until they tasted it. And requested seconds. And the recipe. Janice even posted something about it on her blog saying, "Sounds weird but don't knock it till you've tried it!"

It is such a breeze to make and uses up all of your leftovers. Really. ALL of them.

leftover turkey meat
gravy (leftover and canned if you need more)
mashed potatoes
stuffing
leftover vegetables (add frozen or canned if you need to), chopped into bite-size morsels
Parmesan, grated (as much as you want)
ground black pepper

In the bottom of a large, shallow pan, spread your chopped up leftover turkey meat mixed with your leftover gravy. If you don't have enough gravy just add a can of the premade stuff. You want this mixture to be fairly goopy but not runny. Add a whole bunch of fresh ground pepper and a bit of salt (I like the fresh ground kind as well). Mix in your leftover vegetables. Top with your leftover mashed potatoes and leftover stuffing (if you have any). Sprinkle with Parmesan and bake at 350F for 45 minutes. Serve with a side of cranberry sauce (and a fresh salad) and yes — really and truly — you have used up all your leftovers. If you've got tons of leftovers, make two and freeze one. It'll be great comfort food on a frosty winter's night.

Ham and Bean Soup

Here's another après holiday soup, created with that monster hambone you never know what to do with. And speaking of that bone, rule #1 when it comes to ham: always buy ham on the bone. Always. Not only do you get the bone (and therefore soup) but the flavour is so much better than those ham wedges or chunks or whatever they are. Not as waterlogged. More hammy. I know they're usually huge and unless you are sponsoring a large family gathering, perhaps too huge to consider. Consider regardless. Even if you have lots of leftovers, remove the meat from the bone and freeze it.

Boil up that almost-naked bone the same way you did with the turkey. Water, salt, bay leaves, wine — the whole bit. Remove the bone (let it cool and give it to your dog). Then add your leftover vegetables (if you don't have any add a can of corn or some diced up carrots), potatoes (or not — it's up to you), a whole bunch of fresh ground pepper and 2 large cans of whatever kind of beans you like — baked beans, kidney beans, Romano beans, navy beans, whatever you like. Dump 'em in, sauce and all! And that's the trick. You have to use canned beans because you want that canned sauce in your soup.

And then, for the big cheat: add a can of tomato soup. I find the ham broth to be quite thin no matter how long you boil it, and that magic little can of tomato soup will thicken it up while adding zingy flavour. Let the whole concoction simmer for a few hours, season it up with garlic or basil or whatever you like and you will have a hearty winter soup sure to provide comfort on a frosty January night when you don't have a boyfriend or a dog (yet) and all your girlfriends are busy and your son is with his father and there's nothing on television.

Is that just me?

That Time I Drank A Little Too Much Wine

I MAY HAVE MENTIONED THAT MY HOUSE IS A BIT OF A DROP-IN CENTRE AND, FOR THE MOST PART, MY DOOR IS ALWAYS OPEN. Friends, relatives, my son's buddies, wayward strangers, ex-lovers—they're all welcome. Usually when they show up, I'll cook them something delicious and invite them to stay as long as they need to.

Such was the case when Sharon left her husband. After a few gypsy days on the lam with her two kids in tow, she arrived on my doorstep physically and emotionally exhausted. Jack and I welcomed them with open arms. How could we not? Sharon had no money, no relatives in the vicinity, a teaching job she had ignored for three days and two kids who desperately needed to get back to school and some sort of routine. Jack looked at this as a great adventure. He is an only child and Sharon's son, Josh, only a year younger and his friend, became the instant brother he always wanted. The two of them happily moved into the basement. Sharon and her ten-year-old daughter, Bella, took over Jack's room (it's just a two bedroom house) and the five of us got on with the business of living — and healing — together.

Sharon really needed to decompress. After her recent emotional upheaval she was quite content to let me launder, clean, shop and, of course, prepare meals. She promised a case of wine and, frankly, yes, I am that easy. We spent many evenings at my kitchen counter hashing out her marital woes while the kids played and I created dinner. This was all pretty good for the boys and not even so bad for Sharon and me, but poor little Bella wasn't exactly finding a kindred spirit anywhere in this equation. Thus was born the idea of a baking night — an evening where the two of us would create yummy somethings while her mother sipped wine and cheered on our efforts.

We decided on orange cranberry muffins because — even though that other woman in his life makes them from scratch and I've had hers and they are damn good — Jack says mine are the best he's ever tasted (so there!). We also decided on orange chocolate cake because believe it or not, I actually had a new boyfriend of sorts at that minute. The guy I told Ben about. I say "of sorts" because in hindsight, I'm not sure that Billy was ever really my boyfriend. He just came into my life and hung around (at his leisure) for a while. Billy's birthday was coming up.

I instructed my new assistant to put all the ingredients on the counter.

Accidental Orange-Chocolate-Cranberry Cake

> **1 box chocolate cake mix** (and everything it says you need)
>
> **1 cup orange juice**
>
> **one bar of quality dark chocolate**
>
> **heavy cream (35%)**
>
> **1 orange (for zest)**
>
> **1/3 cup Grand Marnier** (if you're feeling frisky)

And

The Best Orange-Cranberry Muffins of All Time (so says Jack)

> **1 package basic muffin mix (or oatmeal muffin mix if you prefer)**
>
> **1 cup (approximately) orange juice**
>
> **1 orange (for zest)**
>
> **1 cup (or as many as you want) frozen cranberries**
>
> **Optional: 1 cup (or as many as you want) chopped walnuts**

We started with the cake. Mix the ingredients as per the instructions on the box but where it says add water or milk, use orange juice instead. Zest up that orange peel and add half of it to the cake mix too. Bake as instructed.

Pretty easy, huh? Well, it would have been easy if there hadn't been a little more wine than usual that evening. While Bella was happily pouring and mixing, Sharon and I were happily sipping and chatting when I absent-mindedly dumped the cranberries (meant for the muffins) into the cake mix.

Oops.

What to do? Picking them out one at a time seemed like a whole lot of work and then what would we do with them? They'd be coated in chocolate so we couldn't use them for the muffins. I suppose we could rinse them but, like I said, too much work! Bella made her first executive chef decision and we left them in. What the heck!

And thus was born the first ever accidental orange cranberry chocolate cake. Bella's Birthday Bonanza! Well, we weren't about to name it Vickie's Drunken Disaster, were we?

Bake the cake in a Bundt pan. It's all I ever use because you don't have to worry about layers or filling, it looks quite European and it's easy. Oh, and I never grease with butter or shortening — always Pam. Lots and lots of Pam. Spray away, baby!

For the glaze, simply melt the chocolate in the top of a double boiler. I actually don't own a double boiler and never have (Santa, are you listening?) so I just stack one small saucepan on top of the other. You may not want to try this at home. It can be a somewhat dangerous sport and is perhaps better left to the experts and/or the idiots, depending on what you prefer to call me.

Once the chocolate is melted, remove the top pan from the heat, add the cream and the Grand Marnier and stir till it's nice and smooth. Drizzle it directly from the pan onto the (cooled) cake and then sprinkle the top with the remaining zest. Very pretty and very yummy too. And I will tell you, the cranberries make a wonderful addition. The cake becomes even moister with a surprising twist.

The **muffins** are every bit as simple. **Once again substitute the orange juice for whatever liquid is specified. Dump in the cranberries and zest (and nuts) and bake as directed.**

I will admit that sometimes I'm feeling really lazy (or I don't have any oranges) and not particularly zesty and I leave out that part. No worries — both recipes are still darn good!

Sharon and her brood were with us for about three weeks and Jack and I were sad to see them go. It's amazing how much you can learn about friendship and sharing and generosity and love when a seemingly inconvenient situation is foisted upon you. I'm absolutely certain that I gained as much from Sharon's stay as she did.

Billy loved his cake so much he hung around (in his own sporadic not-quite-boyfriend way) for about six months before we both realized that we were not a match made in heaven (what's that other place?). We really were an odd couple, as evidenced by Sharon's initial reaction upon learning we had hooked up.

"What the fuck? Are you fucking kidding me?"

Something like that.

See, Billy can be a sweetheart and Billy is a party-boy and Billy has a place in Southampton (huge selling point) and Billy also likes to work out and therefore has a pretty rocking bod. I didn't realize how important this was to me until after my 29th date with the 29th guy who was more or less in my age-group and more or less looked like beer was his best friend and the gym a distant memory. I witnessed more saggy jowls, jiggling bellies, drooping shoulders and receding hairlines than I can count. Now Billy, whose best friend really *is* beer, had the receding hairline but he also had a mischievous smile. His pecs were pretty mischievous too, a testament to his ongoing love affair with lifting weights. One morning shortly after Billy and I met, Sharon and I were enjoying a latte on a local patio when he came tearing up on his bicycle...shirtless. All shimmery from sweat and tanned from a summer-full of sunshine. All I could think of was *I'd like a piece of that.* Seriously.

Yikes. Obviously I was getting a little shallow when faced with continuous aesthetic deprivation. As we all know, a hot bod does not a successful relationship guarantee and my intellectual and emotional compatibility with Billy was virtually non-existent. We decided that we would be better off as friends. Well, at least that's what I thought. I've somehow managed to stay friends with most of my exes (except for Grover and that is his decision, not mine) but Billy just couldn't do it. His brain only goes in one direction — forward. Forget the past and move on immediately.

Well, okay. Except in my experience, if you don't take the time to properly mourn the death of a relationship, to assess and ponder and discuss it endlessly with your girlfriends, add in a few late-night phone calls to that very same ex who is moving on without a moment's hesitation, if you don't shed even one tiny tear, write a song or two, cry into a few cauldrons of therapeutic soup that you are cooking while listening to every sad song you can find — well, if you don't do any of those things and simply move on immediately, you may be destined to make the same mistakes over and over again.

Maybe.

The other possibility is that you are the smartest person who ever lived. In my next life I want to be Billy. Just seems so much simpler.

Chums Before Bums

YOU KNOW HOW GUYS (USUALLY DUMB ONES) SAY "BROS BEFORE HOES"? With Billy I learned (the hard way) to always choose chums before bums. Girlfriends are forever! Guys? Well just look at my track record!

Shayann was with me through thick and thin in those early dating days. And you know how she is madly in love with mushrooms, right? So I invented Shay's Creamy Mushroom Lasagna. This recipe was born of my desire to duplicate a frozen mushroom lasagna I discovered in my supermarket. *How hard could it be?* thought I. And how delighted will Shayann be? Not only that, it was a cooking/therapy night. You see, I was slowly and begrudgingly coming to the realization that it wasn't ever going to work with Billy.

We had just been on the phone — a rarity for us because Billy liked to talk about "us" about as much as he liked to read books about quantum physics. He finally said, "Vickie, make this quick okay?" There must have been a hockey game on or something. At that moment I knew why we were doomed. Over the months, during sporadic chats about his "past," I had gleaned that Billy has a very specific modus operandi. He doesn't ever break-up with a woman. He just ignores us or pushes us away until we finally break-up with him. That way he can play the victim ("I didn't do nuthin' wrong") and move on guilt-free.

So that night I said through my tears: "Billy, we can't do this anymore and we both know it. But damnit don't you dare go telling all your buddies and your kids that I ditched you. Because we both know this is you ditching me — in your own unique way."

And I hung up. Just like that. I couldn't believe I had the guts — or even the ability — to do it, but I knew it had to get done. Do you think I was getting smarter?

Well maybe, but that's when the floodgates really opened. And it's also when I decided that I had to cook something for Shayann. Just because I was boyfriend-less once again didn't mean there weren't hungry friends waiting to be fed. I still had a purpose in this life and in my kitchen, and so with tissues and wine close at hand and sad songs at full volume I got to work.

Creamy Mushroom Lasagna

---

2 cans cream of mushroom soup

2/3 can of milk or cream

Big splash of white wine

1 can sliced mushrooms, drained

2 cups fresh mushrooms (you pick), sliced thin

1 Tbsp. butter

Montreal steak spice

fresh ground pepper, garlic and basil to taste

precooked whole wheat lasagna noodles

1 cup asiago, grated

1 cup old white cheddar, grated

Optional: 2 cups broccoli (fresh or frozen) or 2 cups fresh spinach, chopped

---

In a large saucepan, simmer the soup and milk with seasonings. Add the wine. Sauté the fresh mushrooms in butter, adding the canned mushrooms and steak spice about halfway through. If you're using broccoli, add it to the soup mix and simmer for another 10 minutes, stirring occasionally. Add the mushrooms to the soup mix and stir. Remove from heat.

Spread a layer of sauce on the bottom of your lasagna pan, add a layer of noodles, more sauce, sprinkle both cheeses and if you're adding fresh spinach, now's the time. More noodles, more sauce, more cheese, etc. Top with a layer of cheese. Bake at 350F covered with foil for 45 minutes, remove foil and broil until cheese is brown and bubbly. Let stand lightly covered with foil for 15 minutes.

Cheater Tip!

Here's a hint direct from the mushroom queen herself: make it a day before and keep it in the fridge until baking. That's exactly what happened on this inaugural mission (we ate it the following night) and the flavours melded together beautifully. Much more so than if you just create, bake and eat all in the same evening. Not that it's bad that way. It's just better after an overnighter in the fridge. You can even make it and freeze it until you need it.

It was a cathartic evening. There I was, once again cooking and crying and coming to terms with the demise of yet another relationship. And then the phone rang. It was Billy. "Vickie, I don't want this. I don't want this to be over. You're an important part of my life and I don't want this to be over."

Boom! We got back together for a few more months and yes, I know — how easy am I? Doesn't take much. Just a few sweet words (or a case of wine). I told him about my new culinary creation and he suggested in his own inimitably selfless way that I save it for the weekend (and him). Nope! No way! Absolutely not! This one's for Shayann. Because no matter what might happen with Billy (and I knew it was only a matter of time), she is in my life forever. And she will always have first dibs on my mushrooms!

Just Desserts
(We all deserve them, right?
Just ask my ex-husband.)

Here are a few of my favourites:

Super Duper Extra Chocolatey Brownies

I USED TO HAVE THIS FRIEND (MY EX-HUSBAND WON HER IN THE DIVORCE) NAMED LOU WHO WAS A BRILLIANT BAKER. I met Lou through one of my full-time radio jobs (when I was on the air live and she was a fan) because my co-host and I used to chat on-air about food we liked. She would hear us, then bake for us and bring her creations to the station. Eventually we met in person and Lou and I became real friends for a bit.

Now when I say friends "for a bit" what I mean is that even though she was initially my fan/friend, when the marital melodrama hit fever pitch she jumped ship. My ship. Not right away, mind you. She played at being impartial, at loving both "sides," at not choosing a team. That is until Grover discovered an email, sneaky bugger that he was. But I guess that's one of the perks of living with your ex-wife while she dates your current girlfriend's ex-husband. Well, that and as you already know, she did his laundry.

This particular email contradicted everything Lou had said to my face. Stuff like "Hey Vick, you and Grover should come for dinner," somehow turned into "We will never break bread with them!" when emailing my nemesis. I say nemesis only because it was Kay's choice, not mine. I would have happily remained friends with my new boyfriend's ex-wife, especially after she fell in love with my ex-husband. Quite frankly, I would have rather stayed friends with her than with Lou. Why this same ex-wife was pissed at me for having an affair with her husband and then actually stealing him away (which of course I didn't, Grover being a grown man and all) remains a mystery.

Okay, I'm kidding again. Of course it's no mystery. The woman had every right to hate my ever-loving cheating guts. I guess I just hoped that once she fell In love with my hubby she might appreciate the irony and lighten up a little. Nope. Seven years in she continued to be not terribly light when it came to me even though she and dear old HBS were known to socialize with her daughters and even Grover (plus his amour-du-jour) on occasion. I was the bad guy after all. Still. Even after I was done and dusted for good by Grover.

Sometimes I found this kinda weird. Mostly when I was feeling sorry for myself. HBS and Kay had fallen in love pretty damn quick. At first some people (who shall remain nameless) thought it was rebound. Or lust. Or revenge. Or all three. But here we were seven years later and their relationship was looking a whole lot like the real thing. Grover (who I thought had been *my* real thing) had promised to love me forever but had changed his mind. So everybody had moved on and I was still consumed with grief about both my marriage and my affair. Had it all been for nothing? When I said forever to Grover, I truly meant it. Whatever HBS and Kay meant — about their marriages or their relationship with each other — no longer mattered. They were happy. They were still together and going strong. Kay still wouldn't speak to me but at least I knew that HBS was being well tended to. And that gave me some peace.

But, Kay's friendship was not an option. And what with all that duplicity from Lou (I guess I'm like a reformed smoker: *I will never lie again so how dare you?!*) I ultimately chose not to exercise my option with her either. Our friendship ended.

But these brownies (yes, I do always find my way back) were pre-melodrama and pre-friendship options. Honestly I'm really not much of a baker only because if I bake it, I eat it and we all know where that ends up. But Lou's brownies were so decadently divine I finally broke down and begged for the recipe. I had a feeling it was going to be some long, drawn-out complicated affair (apparently I'm good at those), with melting chocolate and double boilers and baking powder and cocoa and weird stuff that my pantry has never seen! But I broke down because those brownies were just that yummy.

Lou (stubborn thing she is) wouldn't fess up. She'd always bring them but wouldn't tell me how to make them. Finally, one night after a few too many beers, she coughed up the recipe. Ready?

---

1 box cheapo brownie mix

1 cup chocolate chips

Bake as directed

I'm serious. That's all it was. She added the chocolate chips to the mix and created heaven. These brownies don't even need frosting, not that I'm a big frosting fan anyway. Serve them hot with vanilla ice cream melting all over them and you have my all-time second favourite dessert. Second favourite, you say? What's the first?

Chocolate Profiteroles

I discovered these little gems in France on a ski trip with my darling ex-husband's family during which we stayed in a private chalet with chalet girls. Seriously. Three gorgeous and nubile Australian girls (travelling for their "gap year") at our beck and call to cook, clean or guide us around the mountains. There wasn't very much snow (which was okay because I wasn't very much of a skier back then) but there was always superb food and gregarious company.

And profiteroles. Piled high like the mountains we were living under, drenched in chocolate (like the snow we finally got at the end of our week).

What exactly is a profiterole? I checked *Wikipedia*.

A profiterole or cream puff is a popular choux pastry. Choux paste is baked into small round puffs that are served cold with a sweet filling and sometimes a topping. The term profiterole refers to a filling of ice cream. A cream puff has a filling of whipped cream or pastry cream, however cream containing alcohol is occasionally used. The puffs may be left plain or cut to resemble swans or decorated with chocolate sauce, caramel, or a dusting of powdered sugar. This dessert should not be confused with puff pastry.

Well, *excusez moi.* All I know is that they are better than sex. And to make from scratch? Every bit as complicated. Not that sex is always complicated but you know there are those times when...

Oh sorry. I digress. Francis made them for me one year (for my birthday instead of cake because it's what I wanted and she is a very good friend). Talk about an ordeal! She was at my house so I was able to bear witness. Profiteroles from scratch wouldn't stand a chance with me at the helm. Try this instead.

---

1 carton or box or whatever you can find of frozen cream puffs or profiteroles (just thaw as many as you need). Yes, you can actually buy them!

1 large bar dark chocolate

1/2 cup heavy cream (35%)

vanilla ice cream

Thaw the cream puffs and pile them onto a serving platter like a pyramid. Just before serving, melt the chocolate in the top of a double boiler, adding the cream to your desired consistency. Drizzle it over your mountain and serve with a scoop of vanilla ice cream. It's just about the easiest dessert ever. And my favourite!

As I mentioned, not only did Fran create this masterpiece for me, she never gave up on me. Not even once. And Fran was madly in love with my ex-husband (in that platonic "you made a great choice" way).

Was she happy that we split up? No. Did she condone my cheating? Of course not. Did she condemn me to everlasting damnation? This woman is a committed, practicing Catholic. And no, she did not. Fran never took sides, never lied, always listened, tried to comprehend and is always here for me when I need her. Most importantly, she still believes in my worth as a human being and is happy to break bread with me (even in public!). I'm sure you can appreciate how much this means to me when so many of my other friends ditched my ass when that Pepsi commercial existence (beautiful people living a beautiful life) was no longer intact. When I left my husband, one (now-ex) friend indignantly suggested that I was having a mid-life crisis. I countered that if that were true I would have found a cute boy-toy with a Corvette, not a poor, middle-aged, balding carpenter with a wife. Francis never abandoned me. She acknowledged my turmoil, she applauded my continual quest to seek and learn, and she shared my love of wine and profiteroles!

This is why profiteroles win the #1 spot. Lou's brownies are still damn good though.

Bruce #1, Bruce #2 and Bruce #3 (not necessarily in that order) aka Carrot Pumpkin Spice Muffins

I LOVE THIS QUOTE FROM MIGNON MCLAUGHLIN: "HOPE IS THE FEELING WE HAVE THAT THE FEELING WE HAVE IS NOT PERMANENT."
I mean truly, how could you not love any quote from a person whose first name conjures up thoughts of filets and barbecues and HP sauce and sautéed mushrooms and, well, you get the picture. Honestly, I don't even know if Mignon is a boy or a girl. What I do know is this quote simply yet eloquently sums up hope.

Now you may be wondering what the heck hope has to do with carrot pumpkin spice muffins. And I'll admit I may be digressing here even more than I usually do, but hope has everything to do with the way I cook. Literally. I hope my concoctions will turn out. I hope my friends will like them. I hope I will like them. I hope none of my diners will get botulism and croak.

But hope is also my perpetual state of "being." Like my dog, Shiloh, who lives in hope that I will feed him, walk him, pet him and play with him, I lived in hope that one day Mr. Right (as opposed to Mr. Right Now) would show up on my doorstep and we would cook together happily ever after. Yes, sure, in all the years since Grover trashed my heart there were guys (Mr. Right Nows) — Charlie, Ben, Billy. And lots and lots of meet-and-greets in between.

Then along came Bruce. We met online shortly after my therapist (because sometimes even my beloved chopping isn't enough) suggested that looking for love in this new-fashioned world might just be a numbers game. You see, I was feeling all stupid that I still required a mate. What was wrong with me without a guy? Why was being with a guy so all-fired fucking important? Turns out I ranked my quest for "contentment without a mate" at a less than enthusiastic 6/10. My quest to be happily mated was a more than solid 15/10.

Those damn therapists are so clever.

Have fun with it, he said. Keep on dating till Mr. Right shows up, he said. Go out as often as you like but don't let it consume you, he said. Enjoy your work and your friends and your son too, he said. But just keep on dating. And don't apologize for it. If it's important to you, that's all that counts.

Wow.

I could actually breathe again. It sure seemed like reasonable advice and it's incredible how your therapist's stamp of approval changes everything.

So there I was, feeling very light and free and back online and emailing a man simply because in his photo he was crouched on a beach in front of a beautiful sunset. His written profile didn't say much and he was cute enough but not drop-dead gorgeous or anything. I just knew that sunset was at Lake Huron and, as you know, I have a huge love affair with Lake Huron (Southampton in particular) sunsets. It seemed a good enough reason to email a stranger. Good as any other, I expect.

Bruce responded immediately and within three days we were on our first date.

Now, there are a few things I gotta tell you before I continue this story (*Excuse me?* you're wondering, I know. *What about those muffins?*). See, you already know how pulverized I was by Grover, who I truly believed was the love of my life, and it takes a long time to get over complete pulverization. Not only that, it also takes a conscious effort. Because if you don't consciously deal with the reality (he just wasn't that into me, at least not enough to make it work) that old longing barges into all your future relationships, rendering them damn close to impotent. I think this is why I suffered in a ridiculously disproportionate manner after Billy and I broke up.

Oops. Guess I didn't mention that earlier.

You see, even though I knew Billy was not THE guy for me and even though I was the one who bolted from his cottage and his life,

I fell apart. There were many tears on that very early morning that I departed Southampton. But the sunrise was insanely beautiful so I said, "Okay God, I get it." And I actually did. I got the symbolism. Southampton had always been about sunsets; ergo Endings. On that fateful day it was all about the sunrise; Beginnings. So yes, even though on an intellectual level I understood that I needed to let go of Billy and pursue a new beginning, I sank into a weeks-long depression that I just could not shake. I cried at the drop of a hat, seemingly for no reason, and I simply could not locate my inner joy. On any level. Even chopping and cooking did not help.

I was lonely, plain and simple, and I missed being half of a couple. I also knew enough to realize that however foolish, I was directing that loneliness back to Billy. But it really wasn't about him. It was just the lonely talking. My depression got so bad Cassandra eventually dragged me to the doctor. He suggested anti-depressants, even just for a little while. I'm not opposed to chemical fixes when required but I did not feel any need for that type of help. I wanted to work through this despondency consciously and then somehow banish my melancholy over stupid boys forever.

My disproportionate suffering was not about Billy the Man. It was more about Billy the "Boyfriend." He was the first boyfriend (as in, he met my son and I met his kids and he even slept over sometimes) I'd had since Grover. The first time in three years the actual word "boyfriend" was used. I kinda liked the sound of it, particularly since Grover seemed to have no problem locating girlfriends. At that time I believe he was on #4 or #5. One day on the phone, I asked him, "How do you find girlfriends so quickly?"

"I guess I'm not that picky," he said.

We both laughed about that one.

And I suppose you're wondering what the heck I was doing still yacking with Grover on the phone? Well, in a nutshell (as if), it started when his mother moved and we both ended up helping her at the same time. This was about eight months after he dumped me (for the fourth time) and the first time our paths had crossed since that big dumperoo. At the time he was still on Girlfriend #1. I was feeling good (in the middle of my Charlie phase) and I was having a skinny day (don't you love those?) and a good hair day. We talked, we laughed, we even flirted a bit, we lunched with his mom (with whom I had remained close) and afterward he walked me to my car and we had a huge hug. It felt good.

A few weeks later, around the same time I made my final trip to Vancouver, he dumped GF#1. We ended up on the phone one evening for over an hour and I'm sure that during and after that chat, I had inklings that we might reconnect. You know — romantically. Who else could talk and talk and then talk some more the way Grover and I did? Indeed, he once told me he missed talking with me more than anything. Didn't happen. He was still resolute to get on with his life without me and quickly moved on to GF#2 (he was also doing the online thing).

But yes, we stayed in touch. Grover is a very talented carpenter and had built some pretty beautiful furniture over the years; a few of the pieces were still in my house. About six weeks after he dumped me (did I mention it was for the fourth time?) I moved into my new place. With his furniture. After a year I decided I really should make some sort of cleaner break. Sure, when he moved back into the marital abode he had told me to just keep the stuff for as long as I needed. But how the heck long was that? Till death do us part? I don't think so. Not quite a gift but a kinda generous loan that smacked of "maybe someday you and I and all that glorious furniture will reunite." At least that's how it sounded to me in my grief-stricken, heartbroken state. But after all those months with absolutely zero sign of my fantasy reunion, I was determined to at least attempt some sort of genesis and divest myself of all attachment to Grover and his timbers. Unless the gift was for good (it was damn nice stuff, after all). I finally decided that he had to either A) give me these pieces forever or B) come and get them. It took the boy exactly three seconds to say he'd be right over to fetch 'em — generosity with wooden objects obviously not his strongest suit.

However, even his lack of magnanimity led to our continued interaction, which led to the consumption of wine, then the occasional email, the occasional phone call and one time I even gifted him with two media tickets to a blues festival so that he could take GF#2. Alas (for Grover), even my act of selfless generosity didn't keep them together and soon enough GF#2 was toast and he was working on GF#3. I say "working on" because this particular conquest was apparently playing a little harder to get, which of course made Grover all the more smitten.

How do I know this?

Well, this was during my Ben phase, and one night when Ben bailed on me at the last moment I threw caution to the wind and invited Grover for dinner. To my astonishment, he accepted. It was a surprisingly magical evening. He looked damn good. Slimmer (miss my cooking, eh buddy?) but good. That smile hadn't diminished in the slightest. I looked damn good too (if I do say so myself — and I just did) in spite of the 10lbs I had somehow managed to pack back on (trauma diet be damned!) since our split. Grover had always liked a more voluptuous woman anyway and my boobs were beckoning.

We talked non-stop for five hours. Yes, I said five. He complimented my cooking (curry), my new home (*sans* his wood), the way I looked (nice breasts, Vick) — everything. Our conversational topics knew no boundaries. From kids to love to sex to his potential new GF to Ben to our exes, we talked up one crazy storm. At the evening's conclusion, we had a simple hug and he was gone.

Naturally, I was a little confused but, honestly, mostly just happy. Like I've said, I like to end with friendship, acknowledging that love was there and love was real. And the truth is I just really enjoyed Grover's company. I went to sleep that night smiling.

Two days later he sent me an email. It was so full of vitriol and hostility I was sure the poor man had suffered an accident when he left my house. A serious brain-crushing accident. The words and the tone felt nothing like the lovely evening we had just shared. So, never one to hesitate lest actual reason take over, I called him.

"What's up? What is with that email? I thought we had a great evening. What the heck happened? Did you forget to tell me about the lobotomy you were apparently having the day after our dinner?" (Sometimes I crack myself up.)

"Very funny, Vickie. Ha ha. It was great, honest, but then I woke up yesterday morning and I felt like shit. Like I got hit by a truck. You know, emotionally. I was fucking miserable all day."

"But why?"

"No idea. I was just miserable. Miserable and ornery. I seriously never wanted to see you again. But not just you. I didn't want to see that new girl again either. I don't think I wanted to see anybody ever again. I was just so damn mad!"

"I still don't get it." Yep, I was confused. "What could have possibly happened over curry that precipitated this? Was it perhaps too spicy?" (When in doubt, always go for the laugh, right?)

"I dunno," he sulked (I'm sure he was laughing on the inside). "Do you?"

Well damn tootin' I'm pretty sure I did. "Yes. Yes I do know." It had suddenly become very, very clear to me.

There was a moment of silence after which he murmured quietly, "Okay. I think I do too. But tell me your theory."

And so I theorized. "Okay then. We had a wonderful night. Just like the old days, right? And you know all those complaints you told me about all your recent girlfriends? Like the way the one girl always yelled at her mother? And the way the other girl cut up onions, like she was a little kid afraid to hurt herself? Or the way you always fight about sex and who gets what, when? Well, I don't think any of those problems apply to me. We can talk, right? About anything and everything, right? Endlessly."

I paused, expecting a grunt or a sigh or even an argument. Nothing.

"You like to watch me cook, right? I watched you watching me cook. You like it. You like to eat what I cook, right? And you said my home was beautiful and spotless. And I know you like that."

Still nothing.

One last deep breath and I went for the close: "And you said I still looked good. And sexy. And obviously I still like sex." We had talked a lot about sex.

"So what are you saying?" He finally said without much enthusiasm.

"What I am saying is that I think you left here wondering why the hell we aren't still together. And you woke up the next day wondering the same damn thing and then you couldn't come to terms with it because you can't come to terms with me and what we did and how your daughters hate me and how your ex-wife hates me and so your only choice was to get mad at me and hate me but you don't really so you just decided to hate everybody!"

"Yep. That could be it." His tone was flat as a pancake.

I knew there was also a deeper reason. The really big fat irrefutable reason that Grover and I could not be together: it is impossible to love someone when the very act of loving that person causes you to hate yourself. And Grover hated himself for loving me. He hated himself for hurting his wife and his daughters and destroying (I actually prefer the term "rearranging") their family. He hated himself. The problem with that is, regardless of his self-loathing, he still had to live in his skin. So hating me was the next best thing.

Near the end of our relationship Grover found all kinds of reasons to hate me. Some of them were even justified. I'll tell you, when you're in love with a man who still lives with his ex-wife, who does nothing to facilitate legal separation — even after over two years (my ex and I wrapped that up in about two months!) — who thinks that ex-marital panties have every right to co-flap and who refuses to fight for your love on any level, especially with his daughters...when you're *literally* hopelessly in love with that man, your behaviour tends to go a bit batty. I was batty. I was insecure, emotional, scared and, mostly, I was frustrated. Crazy and a whole lot miffed. I had spent hours since leaving HBS talking with Jack about my right to love Grover. Even (eventually) fighting for his father's right to love whomever he chose (by that time Jack was finding his father's choice unpalatable too). It was all about grown-up love, and I explained over and over again that no one — not even your kids — can tell you whom to love. I reminded him that at some point in his life, Jack would choose to love his own someone and my opinion would not really matter.

I also refused to allow my son to hold me emotionally hostage — ever. There would be none of that sort of blackmail. None of that "I won't love you anymore if you don't do what I want" stuff. I never made him stay with me if he didn't want to (and there were many nights he didn't) and when he (or we) succumbed to screaming, yelling, crying and threatening, I called his father to come get him even though I knew I'd have to endure that "You suck as a mother" smirk.

On the other hand, after that first year of sporadic contact (at best), Grover was gradually moving back into his daughters' good graces, and it appeared that the more he distanced himself from me, the more generous those graces became. I could see that. He loves those girls dearly and their disdain for me certainly spilled over onto him during that first year we were together. After he moved back home in the second year, they lightened up toward him (even though he was still with me). But the line was clearly drawn in the sand. Even his wife told him (and me too, one night on the phone) repeatedly: "The girls will never ever accept Vickie. Ever." So there was poor Grover, loving me, loving his daughters, and knowing pretty much for certain the twain shall never meet.

I beg to differ. All relationships take work. If he wanted his daughters to accept me he would have to work at it and not be held emotionally hostage. But he couldn't risk losing them again, so "separate lives" seemed the only option. He had his other life, the life at the matrimonial home that involved his ex-wife, his daughters, his work and his history. And he had his life with me, with new friends, music, a cozy townhouse and great sex.

He could tolerate it. I hated it.

As a result I acted out far too often (exactly who was the kid here?) and he ended up hating me. Except he really didn't. He loved me. So he ended up hating himself. I get the self-hatred thing. I too experienced horrendous bouts of despair — the kind when waywardly walking in front of a bus seems like a good idea. The upheaval, the guilt, the children's emotions, the guilt, the very real fear that I would lose Grover, the guilt, the guilt, the guilt....

Naturally, I went to Francis about this, and her advice was quite simple: ask them all for forgiveness. Ask the kids, the wife, your husband (I had already asked my son, many times). Ask them all.

"What if they say no?" I queried.

I believe that on some level my husband had already forgiven me because, astute man that he is, he was able to take some ownership of our marriage's demise. So it was really Kay's forgiveness I was looking for, which may have led to her daughters accepting me. But Grover told me she would never ever forgive me. And if she couldn't, how could her daughters?

"So, sure," I told Fran, "I can ask for forgiveness. What if she says no?"

"Then you forgive her," answered my ever-so-eloquent guru. "And let it go so you can forgive yourself."

This seemed like damn good advice, so I took it. I wrote an email to Kay:

> On Saturday night, for the first time in well over two years, I played your song. I finally could. As a result of Friday. Friday was a tear-filled, painful, gut-wrenching, soul searching, emotionally exhausting and frightening kind of day. Yet there were also epiphanies to be had. Good ones. Not good as in fun. But good as in necessary.
>
> The day started with Grover's disclosure of why your younger daughter will never even want to try to accept me. Not just because I broke up her family but because she views me as a duplicitous, phony actress. Someone who thinks nothing of cuckolding her husband. Someone with no concern for anyone but herself. Someone so selfish she would do whatever it takes to get what she wants, damn the consequences.
>
> Guess what? She's right. Epiphany #1.
>
> Well, partially right. But right enough to sting profoundly. I could make excuses and give reasons and beg for understanding for my pain and what I endured and how tortured I was to do what I did but that wouldn't negate the cold hard fact that she is right enough.
>
> I can also protest all I want about "Don't they care about their father's happiness?" but the fact is the girls have every right to hate me. Heck, I hate me. Epiphany #2.

That's a tough one, hating yourself. Actually no, it's fairly easy to hate yourself. All you do is indulge in self-destructive behaviour in the hopes that one day some superior power will strike you down and say, "So there!" The tough part is actually admitting that you hate yourself. Because once you admit that you hate yourself, you either have to lie down in front of a bus or accept responsibility for why and then try to change.

Epiphany #3. No matter how strong our feelings for one another, it is damn hard for Grover and me to carry on. Because too many times we look at each other and are reminded of what we did. Who we hurt. How much we hate ourselves. And how do you love someone else when it is that very act of love that causes self-loathing?

Grover did his self-loathing in the first year after he left you. And during that time, I was so concerned with his self-loathing, and I was so afraid that he would leave me, I couldn't even get close to addressing my own. But now he is more at peace. He tried what he thought he had to try. For whatever reasons, it worked out the way it did. But it allowed him to, in some small way, forgive himself. But for me, it is only now that I can face my own issues. The issues of what I did to you, to your family, to my own. And I feel sick.

In a stupidly ironic catch 22, Grover is the only one who makes me feel better. I look solely to him for reaffirmation. For evidence that I am worthwhile. No, not worthwhile, but worthy. Worthy of love, friendship, joy in my life. All the things that I don't feel worthy of but all the things he brings to my world regardless. Because he has somehow found a way to look beyond my darkness and see more.

But the more the self-loathing increases the more I need this reaffirmation, and the more I look to him for it. The more needy I become. The more demanding. And the more demanding I become, the less he has to give. Because he is overwhelmed with the needs of us all. Wives, kids, parents, homes, work and then...a self-loathing girlfriend who can only find the tiniest modicum of peace when he loves her. It is this very need for his love which drives him away. Epiphany #4.

The therapist said to me months ago, "Vickie, it is time to forgive yourself." So I did. For a day. Funny how this stuff just doesn't go away. I mean damn, I paid my hundred bucks and he told me I was worthwhile and that it was okay to forgive myself and it still didn't happen. I wish I was a bit more religious. Then I could just let God forgive me and be done with it. Not happening. And so I realize that in order for me to find peace and forgive myself it may behoove me to look to the 12 Step Program. Not all of it, but steps 4 and 8. Epiphany #5.

Step 4) Make a searching and fearless moral inventory of ourselves.

See above. I hope it is at least a start. My darling ex told me last summer that the reason you could somehow forgive Grover but not me, possibly in the same way that he can somehow forgive me but not Grover, is that deep down you will take some responsibility for the demise of your marriage. But you will not take any responsibility for what I did to you. Fair enough. I can make excuses for what I did to my marriage based on history, our joint issues and even he can accept responsibility (as he has) for being "emotionally unavailable" to me all those years. But all you ever did was be my friend. And I betrayed that friendship. For that, I must beg forgiveness.

Step 8) Make a list of all persons we have harmed and become willing to make amends to them all.

Well, I think we all know who is on that list. I suppose it could be a very long list so perhaps I need to now concern myself only with the upper echelon. But how to make amends? If I stop loving Grover will that make it better? If I keep loving Grover but stop acting on that love will that make it better? Do I send him off into (eventually) the arms of another woman, a woman his daughters might accept and even eventually love? Is there some type of restitution that can be made? Or is my penance simply knowing that the man I love is the one man I can't be with? Because even if I forgive myself, how can I have a relationship with a man whose daughters will never accept me? Epiphany #6.

Except then I remember — never say never. Because you never (oops) know what will happen. People change, time soothes, hearts open and forgiveness can be had. From self and others. I am grateful to have many family members and dear friends who have already forgiven me. Friday night on the phone, as I drowned in the depths of despair, my friend Fran said, "Vickie, this is good!" "Huh?" I replied hopelessly. "I'm dying here." And she, in her own spiritual way, said, "Now you can ask for forgiveness." And I said, "But I know they won't forgive me." And she said "Then forgive them for that. But at least now you can move on."

And so...I ask for your forgiveness. I can never be sorry for loving Grover, but I am so terribly sorry for the way in which I acted on that love. The moment it was apparent to both of us, we should have walked away. Either to regroup with our families or until we could leave you both honourably and begin anew. I would ask forgiveness of your girls as well, but I find I can no longer inflict myself upon them. It is far too painful for us all. I can only hope that someday, someone will ask for me.

I sang your song on Saturday night to remind myself of what you once meant to me. And to remember that nothing has changed. Because I also look back on that first email I sent you many months ago and am reminded of what I felt...and still feel. Do you remember what I wrote?

"As incredulous as this may seem, please believe that every ounce of affection, every ounce of friendship, every ounce of love I ever showed for you was real. I don't know how I was able to separate these two opposing emotions, my love for Grover and my love for you, but I could. When we (you and I) talked on the phone, attended parties, took vacations, visited one another's homes, whatever — I cherished every moment with you. I loved your heart, your spirit, your sense of humour, your compassion and even your touch of evil. And when I wrote you that song last Christmas, without having any clue what the future might bring, I only hoped that no matter what, you would one day be able to look back on it and know that I meant every word. There is nothing false in those lyrics. Life is complicated...but all I need to know is that there was a time I called you friend."

And so now I take solace in those words. I hope one day you will too. But if you can't...ever...that is your right. I must stop trying to convince you differently.

I am told you can't be in the same room with me and still breathe. Maybe this is much like how I feel ill every time I drive up your lane. But I believe that if just once, you sat in a room with me, looked me in the eye, told me off, spit in my face, whatever...I wouldn't scare you so much anymore. Because you would realize that I am not evil incarnate. I am just a fucked-up girl. Who is as scared, and scarred, as you are. Scarred of my own doing, yes, and for that I take full responsibility. And once again, beg forgiveness. Perhaps if you learned to breathe in the same room as me, life might become easier for Jack. Perhaps not.

The invitation will stand forever. I will buy you lunch, a bottle of wine, a cup of tea. You can come at me with both barrels blazing and I'll take every bullet. Because I deserve them all.

And if you can't right now, or never, and if you simply toss this email in the trash, I will understand, and I will forgive you.

Vickie

I never got a response. And nothing changed. Our relationship continued to dwell in ice and stone.

Okay, back to the call with Grover (I know, there I go digressing again) after our dinner (in case you forgot). My little speech did nothing to change his mood. He might have agreed but it didn't matter. He mumbled something incoherent and then ended the call.

"Thanks again for dinner and good-bye."

Well. It was almost like a fifth dumping. But I was a much stronger girl already and I did not fall apart. At least not immediately.

As for Kay, when Grover did dump me (for the fourth time) she eventually got evicted from their shared abode (as he had predicted). A few years later, when she was living with my ex full-time, I happened to call the house to locate Jack's skis for an upcoming trip. She answered. After her standard greeting (an arctic "Yes?") we somehow got into it. Truly, we are very much alike and neither could resist. Our conversation (as always) went back to what an awful human being I am. I concurred yet again and finally, after listening patiently to her non-stop venom, I took a deep breath and spewed out the bitter truth.

"I have two choices," I said. "Forgive myself or kill myself. Which do you want?"

She knew I wasn't kidding. And she was silent.

The conversation closed abruptly. She certainly wasn't going to suggest suicide and yet forgiveness was too much. The only answer was silence. The upside was that somehow after that call, she became just a little kinder to me. Not friendly, but softer.

And by the way, if you're wondering about the song, it was my Christmas gift to her the holiday before Grover and I confessed. All because she challenged me. This woman is not only a skilled chef, gardener and motorcyclist, but quite an accomplished artist, her medium being intarsia (wood inlay). She also makes super funky wooden Christmas trees (Dr. Seuss style) and that Christmas I had ordered quite the forest. When I picked them up I asked, "What do I owe you?"

She said "Nothing." And then with her uniquely evil laugh added, "Why don't you just make me something?"

I'm sure she thought this was hilarious because my artistic talent ranks right up there with my ability to rebuild a car engine. But she forgot that I could write her a song. And so I did. A few nights before Christmas, with hubbies and children in attendance, I sang it to her and we both sobbed. I from guilt, she from surprise and — dare I say? — love. I hung on to that moment for many months. In fact, I still do. It was a moment of divine friendship and love; one I knew was about to explode into tiny fragments of disgust. But yes, that Christmas it was beautifully real.

Months later in a moment of clarity and generosity, my husband confessed that soon after he and Kay fell in love, he had reminded her of that line in my song: *Life is complicated, full of unexpected twists and bends. You never know where love will take you, you never know when it will end, I'm just glad there was a time I called you friend..."* He got it. The irony, the foreshadowing, all of it. Thank you, HBS.

After that phone call and her subsequent softening, I felt there was hope. Hope for something beyond a relationship built on complete disdain. Because, as I reminded her, she chose to have a relationship with my ex, and therefore with my son and me. For all time. Stuck with us, she was, so she might as well make the best of it.

Okay. Back to the Bruce story, via the Billy story. Seriously? What muffins?

You see, when the Billy thing tanked, I was feeling like a total loser who just can't keep a guy. Now I know this is a pretty stupid way to feel, since I was the one who ultimately pulled the plug on the relationship, but hey — nobody ever said I was smart (one of Grover's favourite expressions, by the way). After Billy, I slipped into a little — okay a BIG — funk and then one day in the middle of my yoga practice (thanks again, Charlie) I realized that I have this *need* to end all my relationships with love. LOVE. To give them worth and validation that in turn validates me. I don't like volatile, door-slamming, dramatic exits (even when I facilitate them). I like to remember the good and learn from the bad.

I like love.

Grover and I never had our closure (with love), and I really wanted it. Thought I needed it. I recognized that my funk was not about Billy and our dramatic ending (yes, I stormed out) but more about Grover and those protracted endings that never ended. I decided I needed closure. Grover closure.

I called him. It had been quite some time since we had communicated. Our most recent ending, one that was precipitated by a ridiculous email that he sent, had not exactly been oozing with affection. You see, I had broken my ankle and called him from the hospital, all hopped up on drugs, on my way to surgery.

"Hey it's me, Vickie. In hospital. Broke my ankle last night. Going to surgery now. You have power of attorney over my body, whatever that thing is called okay, so no tubes or anything if this all goes south. Okay?"

"Whaaaaaat? You did what? You're where? What the hell happened?"

"Ankle broke. Slipped on icy step. Gotta go now. Bye."

And that was that. He called me later that evening but the morphine precluded any sort of meaningful discourse. And then, a few weeks after I returned home (on crutches, absolutely no weight-bearing for six weeks) he called me again. Except this time it was a pocket dial. At least that's what he said.

"Well, now that I have you, how are you doing with that ankle thing?"

"That ankle thing is a challenge. I can't do laundry, I can't vacuum, I can't drive and even making coffee is troublesome."

"Oh come on Vickie, don't be so dramatic. It can't be all that bad? I broke a bone in my foot years ago and I managed."

"Were you allowed to put weight on that foot?"

"Well yes, I could, because I had a walking cast on."

"I can't. No weight. Zero weight. No putting foot down. Ever. For another four weeks. That means crutches and doing the staircase on my ass and did I mention I can't drive?"

"Yeah, so?"

"Kinda makes getting to work difficult. Thankfully they've arranged a limo service for me so I'm good. But I can't go buy groceries and even if I could, I can't carry them and I still need to feed Jack. And myself for that matter. So hey, listen, if you're ever in town grabbing food could you call me and maybe pick up a few things? All of my friends are helping out, which I really, really appreciate."

"Vickie, geez, think about it. I'm busy. I barely have enough time in my life to pick up my own groceries much less become your food delivery person."

Oh. Yes, I suppose that extra five minutes at the market and the extra ten minutes it would take to drop the food off was unimaginable, busy boy that he was. Just to be clear, this was a man who supported Amnesty International and railed against social injustice daily.

"Don't you think it's a bit weird that you are so vocal about international injustice and yet so unwilling to help out a friend in need?" Never one to back away from potential conflict, yep, that's me!

"I gotta go, Vickie. That's a stupid question. And I have work to do. Hope you feel better soon."

A few days later he sent me an email. Now I really must preface this story with a wee disclaimer. At first it will sound sordid and disgusting.

But I urge you to read on because there is most definitely method in this madness. What Grover wrote to me went something like this:

While you are recuperating from your injury you may have time to ponder this question: is it ever appropriate and acceptable for a grown man to put a baby's penis in his mouth?

What the fuck? What the fucking fuck? I was flabbergasted.

But before you go getting your knickers in a knot, it's vital that you understand Grover. He is not a deviant or sicko, and he is absolutely "normal" in the sex department. He *is* a voracious reader and an enthusiastic learner. Truly one of the most learned men I've ever met because everything interests him. Knowing this, I immediately concluded that he had probably read a *National Geographic* article about some ancient pygmy tribe and their ritual of whatever, whatever, whatever. This was not a sex question or a pedophile problem. This was Grover being a shit-disturber. A provocateur. This was Grover feeling bad about not helping me out, so he disturbed some shit to make himself feel better. I'm sure he was expecting me to freak out on him at which time he could call me a lunatic and then innocently explain to me what he had read. I *knew* him.

I wasn't about to play along. Hey, you want to provoke? Hold my beer. I responded to his email:

Interesting question. Perhaps I'll forward it to your wife and daughters and they can weigh in? Or maybe I should send it to Shayann's pal the cop who works in child pornography? Or next time I have lunch with your mother I'll ask her? Seriously. I know you. You're just trying to get a rise out of me. You've learned some weirdo fact about something somewhere and instead of just sharing it like a normal person you're trying to provoke me. So that you can then swoop in and tell me that I'm crazy and volatile and it's really just about the pygmies. Or something. I am not playing.

I was so damn proud of that reply. I knew it wouldn't score me any points, but it had to be said. Shit-disturbers love to disturb shit and I just didn't have the energy for more disturbance.

Didn't take long for his reply to come blasting in:

> Vickie, have you lost your fucking mind? My daughters? A cop? Are you fucking crazy? I merely read an article about a rabbi in New York City who gave two babies herpes because part of some ancient bris ceremony involves pulling the foreskin off with their mouths.

Something like that.

I looked it up on *Wikipedia*:

Metzitzah B'Peh (oral suction)

The ancient method of performing metzitzah b'peh (oral suction) has become controversial. The process has the mohel put his mouth directly on the circumcision wound to draw blood away from the cut. The majority of Jewish circumcision ceremonies do not use metzitzah b'peh, but some Haredi Jews use it. It has been documented that the practice poses a serious risk of spreading herpes to the infant.

Well, yay Grover. What a clever boy. I didn't care. The conversation ended.

So did my friendship with his mother. She called me tearfully a few days later. We had planned a dinner together and I was looking forward to an evening in her company and her divine cooking. Alas, it was not to be.

"I don't know how to tell you this my dear Vickie," she whispered in her soft, lilting German accent.

She was in obvious distress. "Anna, what's wrong? Are you okay? Did something happen?"

A few more sighs. "I'm okay my dear. I mean, not really but nothing happened to me. Except...." More tiny sobs. I was getting really concerned.

"Just breathe, Anna. And then spit it out. It's okay, whatever it is." I had a strong suspicion this had something to do with Grover and his email. I had told her about it and she was dismayed and very angry with him.

"Okay, I'll tell you. We were having dinner Sunday. My son and his new girlfriend and the others. And I asked him what had possessed him to write that stupid email to you. Quietly, you know. Not in front of everyone."

There it was. My gut told me where this was going.

"And then he pulled me aside and said he doesn't want me to be friends with you anymore."

And she burst into a full symphony of tears. Wow. I was shocked and not shocked. Nothing Grover did shocked me anymore. And I was tired. Tired of hostile interactions and tired of caring.

"Now listen to me, Anna, you need to stop crying, okay? You know how much I love you but I will not come between a mother and her son. Grover is your son. You must put him before me."

I suppose I was being altruistic, but maybe I was also being a little selfish. My continued connection to Grover's parents (his father and I socialized too) kept me continually connected to him. It was no doubt better for me to cut that cord. Any connection to Grover was detrimental to my emotional well-being and my ability to get on with my life

"But I enjoy your company so much, Vickie. I just don't know what to do!"

"Yes you do." It was my turn to sigh. "Blood is thicker than water, Anna. You must be true to your blood."

There was a long pause. I almost thought our connection had broken. "I will miss you so very much, my dear."

"And I you. More than you know."

And that was that. The end of our friendship. The untethering of me. I have not spoken with her since.

So, back to that phone call — the one I hoped would lead to closure. (I know, I digressed again. I just think you need to know this stuff.) Grover answered on the third ring. He was surprised, nervous, shaky voice and all.

"Hey Vickie. How are you?"

"I'm okay I guess. Or not. I dunno, maybe not so okay."

"What's up?"

"I think I'm having a hard time with my life, you know. Just sorting through what happened and why and where to go from here and I was just thinking that maybe if you and I got together for a glass of wine we could get ourselves to a better place. Like, with each other."

Silence.

"Um, like a place where we can acknowledge that what we had was special and what we felt was real and maybe we can smile and shake hands and kinda leave it with love. Ya know what I mean?"

Long pause.

"Um, yeah, I guess I kinda do. Sort of," he said. "But things are going pretty good for me right now. And I don't think I can do that. Plus my new girlfriend wouldn't like that."

"Bring her along! Seriously, I'd love to meet her. This is not about sneaking around or us getting back together. This is about closure — with love. What is so wrong about closure with love?"

I don't think he got it. Grover is an extremely bright and inquisitive guy, but only when the topic interests him. He loves to share his knowledge, as often as possible, with whoever will listen. Even my son (smarty pants) once bought Grover a T-shirt that said, "Everyone Is Entitled to My Opinion." But this was not a subject Grover cared to face. I was the perennial sore spot, best left to fester in the past.

And just so you know — the past wasn't all bad. In the three years we were together Grover and I enjoyed some truly magical moments. A trip to St. Martin (the French side) and St. Bart's where we frolicked naked (and semi-naked) and he bought me a beautiful silver ring. A trip to the local park for a brisk morning walk (before breakfast and sex). A trip to New York City because Christmas in New York was on my bucket list. We skated in Central Park, saw the Rockefeller tree and got drunk on green apple martinis at the Carlisle. A trip to a local bistro where we sat side by side and shared every course (between kisses). A trip to Virgin Gorda because Grover had kept a copy of *Life* magazine (dating back probably twenty-five years) with a picture of a woman bouldering there. Grover was a climber who really wanted to boulder there. So we checked off his bucket list item too. A trip to Boston where we stayed with my cousin who lovingly billed it our "honeymoon" because we spent so much time in the bedroom. A trip to the gas station to fill up the tank and kiss passionately while doing it. That's how we rolled, Grover and I. Almost everything we did together was a great adventure. I suppose that is one of the upsides of being madly in love.

Of course the downside is the "madly" part; insanity never, as a rule, results in good health. And now here we were, three years post-final-breakup and it appeared that this man I had adored whole heartedly — to the detriment of everyone around me — wasn't particularly interested in giving me closure, a glass of wine or even a coherent conversation. He kept muttering and sputtering and suddenly it hit me. I was done! Done with my quest for a "happy ending." Done with my need to close with love. Done with my desire to gain understanding and peace. It hit me that Grover didn't need loving closure because loving me on any level would just mess him up all over again. Hostile-cum-silent closure suited his needs much more because with it he could keep hating me, blaming me and forgiving himself. He needed something much different to survive.

Either that or he just didn't give a shit.

It was a big, fat growing-up moment for me and when I hung up that phone I felt free. I suddenly felt free to live my life my way, no longer shackled to Grover and the misguided hope that he might still end up being the love of my life.

So — and here's where we get back to the real story — it was the very next day that I spoke to Bruce for the first time. The very next day! You remember Bruce, right? The sunset guy? Title of this chapter? Pumpkin spice muffins? I know, I know, it was a long time ago. Yes, Bruce and I spoke and I felt like I had known him my entire life. There was none of that first call awkwardness or formality. He was funny and witty and aggressive, which is so darned attractive to me because I'm not exactly a wallflower and some guys get, um, intimidated. Not Bruce. He gave as good as he got and life was suddenly one big non-stop smile. It was so natural and easy and we went full-on right from the start. And we kept full-on (calls, texts, emails) until a few days later when we had our first date.

I read an article somewhere that purports a woman can ascertain within the first three minutes of meeting a man if she would kiss him. Not that she necessarily will, just that she could. Well, forget the knowing. Bruce and I were kissing within three minutes. Little kisses that grew up into big ones way too fast. By the time we got to dessert (at a restaurant, thank you very much) we were kissing in public and not caring who saw. It was all pretty damn good. And I don't just mean the kissing. I mean the talking and the laughing and the connecting. I cancelled the other two dates I had lined up (hey, my therapist told me to play the numbers) and Bruce and I embarked on our adventure.

In the first two months we had some pretty wonderful moments, and I was feeling the most optimistic I had in a very long time. We seemed like twin flames, Bruce and I. Both flawed, both with colourful histories, both with many mistakes and regrets chalked up, and yet, both smitten. Or so I thought.

He really loved my cooking too. He even gained 10lbs, which he could certainly stand, since he'd been on the trauma diet in the months leading up to our fateful rendezvous. You remember the trauma diet? The one where you're so screwed up you just can't eat? You see, Bruce's marital situation (he'd been separated for less than five months when we met) was so complex and sad and guilt-ridden, it made my former soap opera look like a Disney movie (at least my ex got his happy ending). But Bruce's wife was ill with an incurable condition and he was bitter. Confused, guilt-ridden and bitter. Plus he had recently come out of an extra-marital liaison that had pulverized him. Yes, in the final years of his marriage he had an affair and she had broken his heart. His pain was far fresher than mine.

This all created a bit of a dual-personality Bruce. One night after playing in a golf tournament, he called me. He was tipsy (bordering on drunk as a skunk).

"Hey shcweetie, iz me. Brucie. Howz the prettiest girl in Guelph tonight and geez I miss you *hic* really super a lot."

"Hi Bruce. Let me guess. You had a few on the course today?"

"Chust a cuppla beers maybe and some wine at dinner and I think some rum. Maybe two."

Maybe ten?

"Anyhoo I chust wanna tell you you're fucking awesome."

"Thank you, Bruce. I think you're awesome too."

"I love you, baby. I really do."

And there it was. Those three magic words. I wasn't expecting them at that moment and I sure as hell wasn't expecting them to be delivered in a drunken ramble. Not the first time. Not any time!

"Bruce, honey, let's not do this right now, okay? Let's do it tomorrow when I see you in person. Go back to your party. Don't drive anywhere! And I'll see you tomorrow, okay?"

"Okey-dokey baby-doll schnookums. Nighty-night. Don't forget to dream about me."

I didn't know what to make of all of this. I liked the affection. I like that he missed me. I guess the drunken goofball was kind of cute. And God knows I was more than ready to fall in love. I decided to just smile about it and wait until the following evening.

He arrived promptly at 5. We drank some wine. We chatted about his golf game. We laughed about his tipsy phone call. We did some serious kissing and laughed some more. That's when I decided it was time to address his "confession."

"So Bruce...about what you said on the phone last night."

"What did I say? I hardly remember a thing," he chuckled.

"You know, the love thing."

"The love thing? What love thing?"

"You honestly don't remember?"

"Um...I remember talking to you. I remember you told me I was drunk. I remember thinking you were probably right. I do not remember any love thing."

"You said 'I love you' Bruce. Like, to me."

Silence.

"You told me you loved me."

Big grin. "No way, Vickie. No way I said that. You're dreaming. I never would have said that."

"But you did."

"No way. I mean I really like you and I like what's happening here but I'm not there yet. No way. There's no way I said that."

Well. I know what I heard. But how the hell could I argue?

It happened one other time, again when he was drunk. That time he told me in person after a long evening of boozing it up with friends. I let that one go. Tipsy confessions were obviously his thing. Even if he denied them the next day.

His final drunken confession, though, was a zinger. And it turned out to be undeniable. We were sitting at my kitchen table after dinner (and way too much wine).

"Ya know what, Vick...I gotta tell you the truth. You're a great gal but I think maybe we're just kinda two ships, you know, passing in the night."

"Really?" Eyebrow raises. "I thought you wanted a relationship? You told me on our first date you wanted off that dating site. You said it would be great if we got off that dating site together."

"Did you?" he asked, looking mighty sheepish. "Did you get off the dating site?"

"Of course I did! Didn't you?"

I had been very clear on our first date. I wasn't looking for a fling. I wasn't looking for something casual. I was looking to mate for the rest of my life.

"Um, well, I guess the answer is no. No. I'm still on it."

We had been seeing each other for two months. Seeing each other a lot. I had met his daughter and he had met my son. And he was still shopping online?

"But it's not that," he continued, pouring himself another glass. "It's that other woman I told you about. The one in the States."

"The one you had the affair with?"

"Yeah, her. Cause you see, we're still in touch sometimes."

He had told me they were done. She had gone back to her husband.

"Still in touch how?" I had stopped drinking. I had almost stopped breathing.

"Like she sends me cartoons and funny stuff. Nothing heavy. But she's still there. You know, in my head. I guess I still love her. I don't fucking know..."

Wow. It looked to me like Bruce was pining. Not for his poor infirm ex-wife but for the secret lover who had recently dumped him (but only once, thank you very much). And I'm pretty sure when the party of the first part (him) is still pining, the party of the second part (me) doesn't stand a chance. Because you can't compete with a ghost. The ghost always wins, hindsight being rosy and all that.

It was a tiny little huge frigging fact that I wish he had shared with me earlier in our relationship. But I get it. I hadn't exactly been sharing sordid details of my relationship with Grover or with any other suitor. You feel pathetic and humiliated. Not exactly character traits you're hot to advertise to your potential new love. But of course the double-edged sword was that Bruce's secret was rendering our relationship impotent. He knew it all along. He just didn't tell me.

So there we were, crashing and burning. We didn't give up though. Not that night and not right away. We really did have some kind of weird "soul" connection. But finally, after a few tumultuous weeks he broke up with me officially (although he called it a timeout). He needed some space. He needed to sort through stuff. He probably needed to call the girl in the States.

I decided to escape to Southampton. It was Thanksgiving weekend and I was desperate for a sunset, the sound of waves and some solitude. Bruce called the first morning I was there. He wanted to chat. Wanted to make sure I was okay. He was visiting the drive-through of the local coffee shop and BAM — he ordered a pumpkin spice muffin!

You thought I was never gonna get to the recipe, didn't you?

He raved about that muffin so much, I thought heck, if I can cheat with orange cranberry and men, how hard can pumpkin spice be?

Turns out it's actually quite simple, cheating pro that I am.

Pumpkin Spice Muffins

half package carrot muffin mix

1 cup canned pumpkin

3/4 cup water

2 Tbsp. pumpkin pie spice

Mix all the ingredients and bake as instructed. Whoever said it's hard to cheat? Well it kinda is sometimes because I tried this one first with oatmeal muffin mix (the only thing in my pantry). The muffins weren't awful but the oatmeal sort of overwhelms the pumpkin, so what's the point? I dashed off to the market to buy plain muffin mix but they didn't have any so carrot seemed the next logical choice. It works beautifully. The spices in the muffin mix blend perfectly with the pumpkin pie spice. And maybe best to start with 1 Tbsp. spice and then keep adding and tasting. Both Jack and I like the zing (he gives these two thumbs up!) but as you know, it's all up to you.

So, back to Bruce. I guess the upshot is he was not ready for a relationship. He wanted to sew wild oats. Maybe he still needed to pine for lost love? Maybe he just wasn't that into me? Maybe I really am a first-class pain in the ass? Whatever the reason, my heart ached for him. Sometimes he was so damn cocky you wanted to cook him up with some red wine. Other times he was such a tortured soul he literally cried out for help, calling himself a "loser."

He wasn't a loser.

But I do believe he was a sieve. Isn't every boy like some kitchen appliance? I mean I know I've dated freezers (icy hearts) and microwaves (fake heat, way too fast) and blenders (keep you churning non-stop) and crock pots (or is that crack pots?) who just simmer endlessly and never get to a boil. Bruce was a sieve. He just kept springing leak after leak and whenever he did he tried to plug up that hole with a Band-Aid. Another girl, another sexual conquest, another drink, even buying another new something. I thought only girls did this (sorry for being sexist) but Bruce likes to shop and it's usually expensive, brand name, show-offy things. Things that help him feel good about himself (outwardly) for a moment, until he feels bad about himself (inwardly) again, because my guess is he always will. Until he addresses the source of the holes in his life and plugs them, he'll keep springing leaks. And until he exorcizes that ghost-girl for good, he will desperately need to keep plugging up the holes. I know this because I lived this.

Every well-equipped kitchen needs a sieve. A well-equipped heart has no need to be one. And I sure as hell don't know how to fix one. And there you have it. Bad analogy and all, my ultimate psycho-babble-cook-cum-armchair-therapist take on yet another relationship gone sour.

Back to the kitchen I went. The beautiful thing about cooking without a recipe is that you can keep tweaking and inventing and re-inventing until one day you get it right! There is so much good in Bruce, and I can only hope he'll do the same.

The sad thing is he never even tried one of the muffins!

Let's Talk Tofu (And Two More Bruces)

OKAY, I KNOW THAT JUST SEEING THE WORD "TOFU" IS PROBABLY COMPELLING YOU TO SURGE FORWARD TO THE NEXT CHAPTER. Truth be told, a few years ago I most certainly would have closed this book myself and gone for a nap. Tofu? Are you kidding me? Tofu tastes like a sponge. Not that I've ever eaten a sponge, but in my mind tofu tastes like sponge imagined.

Then I met Bruce. Yes, another Bruce. As a matter of fact this was just a few weeks after Bruce #1 and I had finally parted company for good. And I guess I should tell you for the sake of clarity that this new Bruce was actually Bruce #3.

Are you still with me?

Bruce #1 (just before pumpkin spice Bruce) was a one-date wonder and probably the biggest disappointment of my online dating career. Here's what happened (I'd like to say "in a nutshell" but I think you know me better than that by now).

He contacted me. Turns out he lived on Lake Huron, a few hours south of my heavenly Southampton, but he at least knew the attraction. He was too old for me. Quite frankly most guys my own age are too old for me so eight years older is way too old for me. But he was quite handsome and a fantastic writer. We shared some poetic emails, some exciting phone calls and a week later our initial meet-and-greet was planned for the first night of my solo week-long Southampton rental cottage getaway. Jack was on summer holiday with his father, I was recovering from some minor surgery, and Bruce was willing to drive north if I was willing to cook for him. I even offered him the bunkie to sleep over and we agreed that there would be no hanky-panky on that first date. Just dinner, a beautiful sunset (I hoped) and an opportunity for low-stress getting-to-know you. We both felt incredibly optimistic. Maybe this would be it? The chemistry on paper and phone was incredible. Maybe the age thing wouldn't be a factor? Maybe this was destiny?

The night before our date, the cottage owner (Larry) informed me there was a water issue at the cottage and he would be there the following day to fix it. Perhaps I wanted to postpone my arrival by a day?

"No way!" said I. "I have a friend meeting me. We'll make do with whatever." I wasn't about to postpone destiny.

I arrived at the cottage and met Larry in the throes of a plumbing party. Shiloh and I moved in, I beautified a bit and started preparing dinner. Homemade cheeseburgers (by request) and one of my famous salads. There I was, sipping wine, nervous and excited about my upcoming date. And all the while chatting it up with Larry (knee deep in wrenches and pipes), who, as it turns out, was a fan of my radio show and quite a bit of fun.

Now speaking of wine, Bruce had mentioned that he wasn't much of a wine connoisseur; he was more of a brandy drinker. That should have been a dead giveaway right there. Who the heck is just a brandy drinker? I mean, I know people who have a brandy after dinner, but I'm pretty sure I've never encountered anyone who only drinks brandy! But I was still enraptured by the poetic emails and flirtatious phone calls, so when he asked what type of wine he should bring for me I ignored the brandy thing and sweetly replied, "Oh, anything will be fine." That is so not like me. Anything is not fine. I strongly dislike Chardonnays, especially the heavily oaked kind (might as well suck on a picnic table) and sweet Rieslings aren't my favourite either. I'm a little easier to please in the red department although I do find that certain cheaper table wines taste like yeast. I have learned to love Canadian Baco Noir and I also love a bold Chianti. But for some reason I did not specify any of that to Bruce #1. I just said *whatever*. I am never at a loss for wine and I didn't want to appear too picky.

Bruce arrived. We had a big hug at the door and he even attempted a tiny peck. And you know how within three minutes a woman knows if she'll kiss a guy? Within three minutes I knew that this was never going to work out. Never ever ever. His skin looked like it was made of wax. I'm not sure how else to describe it, but you would have thought the man had never seen a ray of sunshine in his life. He was downright pasty. And he had so much goop in his full head of gray hair that it wouldn't budge in a hurricane. He was wearing a short-sleeved dress shirt (tucked into his jeans) that looked like something my father would have worn thirty years ago. No, we are not talking vintage. He was all smiley and happy and immediately poured himself a glass of brandy, that bottle being the only thing that entered my cottage with him. I kept waiting for the wine he had promised, but it never materialized.

In the meantime, Larry was still plugging away at the plumbing so I invited him to stay for dinner. What was I supposed to do? Let the poor man starve while Bruce and I ignored him whilst feasting outdoors? I'm not built that way. I wanted water in the cottage and, truth be told, I was beginning to think Larry was more fun than Bruce. Bruce seemed shocked that I would invite "the plumber" to join us, but what could he do? My rental cottage, my dinner. It was a lovely evening that promised one of Southampton's glorious sunsets over the sparkling waters. Even though I was feeling very uncertain, I figured I had no choice but to make the best of it.

"Hey Bruce, do you want to do the barbecue honours?" I ask brightly, hoping to somehow include him in the process. He was hovering around me like a ravenous dog, and I was feeling uncomfortable. I am perfectly capable of grilling burgers but isn't that supposed to be a manly thing, roasting flesh over a flame? I was trying to be nice, to offer up a chance.

Bruce stared at me in disbelief. "I thought you said *you* were going to cook me dinner?" He was serious.

Okaaaay. "Yep, I am. No problem." I'm pretty sure my eyes were rolling so I turned away and opened up the barbecue lid.

Bruce just about fainted. "Are you kidding me? Oh my goodness gracious Vickie, really? How could anyone possibly cook on that monstrosity? It is filthy! I suggest you get that cottage owner over here pronto and insist he purchase a new one."

Huh?

"Um, Bruce...that's why God invented barbecue brushes. You crank up the heat, burn off the old crap and then brush it away."

"No way. No effing way." Geez, how men who cannot say the word "fuck" annoy me. "This filthy beast will at the very least require paper towels and soap and disinfectant and who knows what else!" I'm sure if he could have *harrumphed* he would have. He stomped off into the kitchen, I assumed to find the necessary supplies.

I began wondering how to politely ask him to leave before dinner. I had absolutely no idea how I was going to endure a meal, let alone a night and maybe even breakfast with this man. If there's one thing you may have figured out about me by now, I'm not terribly anal. I live much like I cook — by the seat of my pants. I like a reasonably clean house and a reasonably clean barbecue but I also like to have fun and have learned that anal people are usually too busy being anal to have fun. And Bruce was anal times a hundred.

Eventually, I finished barbecuing the burgers, I readied the table (which was overlooking the lake in anticipation of that spectacular sunset), and the men sat down. I went back to the kitchen to retrieve the salad. Except I couldn't find it. I'd made it about an hour earlier and just left it sitting on the counter. It was gone! I couldn't believe it. Did someone steal my salad? And then I looked in the fridge. There it was. Bruce had put it in the fridge because he didn't want it to "go bad" sitting on the counter. I have made a lot of salads in my time. And many of those salads have sat on my counter for way longer than an hour (you know how it is when the wine gets flowing and you keep putting off dinner?) and no one has ever died. No one has ever even puked. Not in Brucie's world. Brucie with the waxy skin, rock-hard hair, ugly shirt, bad manners (no wine?) and clean freak obsession had put my salad in the fridge.

So we ate. Larry and I chatted and laughed and enjoyed the food. Bruce sat at his end of the table like a sullen brat, picking at his burger, silent and obviously perturbed. I ignored him. I was hoping for a miracle — you know, the kind where he just suddenly vanishes into thin air. No such luck, but Larry did have to vanish ("Please don't go!") for a moment for a chat with the neighbours.

I started to clear the table. Bruce didn't budge. Just sat there sipping his brandy and scowling.

"You know what, Vickie. It deeply saddens me to say this but it appears to me that you are on a date with Larry, not me. I'm finding your behaviour to be quite rude."

Me? Rude? I was speechless. As I stood there, plates in hand, desperately hoping for some clever comeback to magically escape my lips, he announced, "I do not think this is going to work."

Oh my goodness, if relief was audible you would have heard mine across the lake in Michigan! Without further ado (and trying not to smile too broadly) I placed the dishes back on the table. "You know something, Bruce...I think you're right. And since it's not going to work I really don't see any point in you staying the night."

"Of course not! I shall leave right after I've finished this drink."

I, being ever the caring and concerned soul, had another suggestion. "You know I really don't think that drinking and driving is a good idea so maybe right now would be better?"

I couldn't believe I said it, but I was oh-so very glad I did! I could not tolerate another moment. He took the hint. I walked him to his car and when he opened the hatchback to load up his brandy, lo and behold if there wasn't a huge bouquet of fresh flowers — in a vase — tucked into the corner. Now I was truly incredulous. Okay, maybe no wine, but who in the world brings flowers to a first date and leaves them in the car? What was he going to do — check me out first? See if I was worth it? Hightail it outta there with his flowers if I didn't cut the mustard?

Apparently.

"Nice flowers," I laughed. "Who are they for?"

"Obviously not you. Not anymore."

And that was that. He drove off without another word and I can tell you emphatically that in my entire dating career I have never been so happy to see someone leave. Bu-bye!

Larry and I enjoyed the rest of the evening immensely. He couldn't believe that Bruce left, but he didn't care much. The sunset was a beauty, the conversation flowed, we didn't care about the dirty barbecue and no one died from the salad. I rented Larry's cottage many times thereafter, sent him a few new renters, and he and his wife are still friends of mine to this day.

So, now that I've covered Bruce #1 and Bruce #2, let's get back to Bruce #3 — and tofu. After Bruces 1 and 2, I was pretty sure I was done with Bruces forever. I mean really, how many can there be? And in the same year? Then I met the Captain (online of course). There he was in his photo, standing on his sailboat, cheeky smile and a hot pink T-shirt. Big strong arms and a hot pink T-shirt. Soul patch (you know, the tiny little tuft of beard directly under the lower lip) and a hot pink T-shirt. I am a sucker for all of these things so I fired off a quick note: "There is nothing sexier than a man in a hot pink T-shirt." It's true, isn't it? A man confident enough to wear pink is truly confident.

He wrote back and his subject line was "My first time to you." I was instantly intrigued. That one little line was filled with so much optimism. My "first" time. In other words, there will be many more. He made a bit of small talk and then the signature: Bruce. There it was in all its glory. BRUCE! What are the fucking odds? I was blown away and almost decided to end all communication then and there. My Bruce track record was not exactly golden. But there was still that beautiful hot pink shirt which, as it turns out, was actually red. Oh well, reckoned I, what can a few emails hurt?

We corresponded. We spoke on the phone. We did the regular getting-to-know-you dance. Bruce is a scenic carpenter in Toronto. That means he lives about an hour away from me and builds sets for movies and television. Very cool. Obviously, I have a soft spot for the artistic type. Bruce also loves motorcycles and old VW vans (he had one named Fifi). Also cool. I love a road warrior (because I love road trips). And Bruce had just finished living on his sailboat for the entire summer. Actually, beyond summer. Almost till November! He lived on his sailboat — like, his full-time address — at a marina in Toronto. Damn, how cool is that! I have always imagined that living on a boat would be divine. I mean, I didn't know how feasible it would be (thus my love affair with cottages and sunsets) but the dream? Wow. And here was Captain Bruce actually doing it.

And just so you know, I never called him "Captain." Not to his face. But I had to figure out some way to differentiate him from Bruce #2 on my cell phone (Bruce #1 was long banished).

So there he was — outside the box, six feet tall, athletic, artistic and adventuresome — all attributes that are right up my alley. Except for his stupid name, he was looking pretty good. But then we got to the nuts and bolts of who we really are, which is when the waters under this new sailboat got a little choppy. Bruce doesn't drink. Not a drop of alcohol touches that boy's lips nor does he eat anything cooked with alcohol. Are you kidding me? You already know that I not only cook with alcohol (in the glass in my hand) but it usually manages to splash its way into whatever it is I'm making (save for baked goods). I've never met a sauce, stew or soup that wasn't in some way bettered by a healthy squirt of wine. But Bruce doesn't drink. Hasn't for over thirty years for no other reason than he decided he wanted to be as healthy as possible. So healthy in fact, he told me he was planning to live to be 100. Which is why Bruce doesn't drink coffee. Or tea. Or anything caffeinated. Or anything hot for that matter. I don't know about you but I'm one of those need-my-coffee in the morning people. First thing, please. Preferably before anybody even breathes.

And then there's meat. Or I should say there is no meat. Bruce is also a vegetarian. Not vegan, mind you (thank God, because I would literally die a miserable and crabby death without cheese) but no meat, no poultry, no fish. No cheeseburgers, no chicken flatbreads, no lobster on Valentine's Day and no stuffed trout with mango dressing. Not even a tuna sandwich. So, we have a vegetarian non-drinker who wants to live to be 100. My grandmother lived to be 103 (and she loved her fatty meats) and my mother to 93, so I figure I've got some good DNA somewhere.

Which leads us to the offspring issue.

Bruce — an absolutely astonishing fifty-one who looked no more than forty (damn him and his healthy living) — has been married twice but has no children. Never wanted any, thank you kindly. His first marriage ended because his once like-minded wife changed her mind and succumbed to the clanging of her biological clock. I guess she hoped he would too but there was no mind-changing for the Captain.

No kids, no thank you. His second wife already had three daughters when they wed. Teenagers. I guess they weren't such a big issue during the courtship phase but after the nuptials when cohabitation commenced these girls apparently proved themselves to be quite the handful. More than a handful — they were the reason for the end of the marriage. He told me that when they split up, Wife #2 said, "You don't like my kids!" He eloquently replied, "Who would?" Okay, so maybe not the most sensitive response ever muttered but I will admit I laughed, insensitive schmuck that I am.

So, add it all up. The man doesn't drink booze, doesn't like coffee, doesn't eat meat and doesn't want children. I am a certifiable lush, can't start the day without java, love to rip flesh from a bone, and have one adorable child who ain't going anywhere. As I previously asked, what are the fucking odds?

Still, you may have noticed my penchant for masochism and willingness to try just about anything once, so Bruce #3 and I went on our first date. He drove to Guelph and we had dinner at an Indian restaurant. I let him order (except for the wine and yes, I had two glasses without shame) and I was reminded how good everything tasted and how I didn't really miss flesh at all. Bruce is a very attractive man so the view was nice. The conversation was...okay. Easy enough. Well, I should clarify and say easy enough for me. I certainly wasn't having any trouble running off at the mouth and when I eventually realized I wasn't letting the poor boy get a word in edgewise I stated quite emphatically, "That's it! I'm not talking anymore!"

Bruce thought that was hilarious. Because he had already figured me out well enough to know that the odds of me shutting up for any length of time were about as good as the odds of him cracking open a Budweiser. "No don't. Please, Vickie, don't stop talking." He was now grinning ear to ear. "I like that you are a talker."

You know what? I liked that he liked my talking. Most guys like my shutting up.

"Okay then I'll keep talking. But first you need to propose a toast!"

He raised his water glass and somewhat bashfully offered, "Here's to the beginning of a beautiful friendship."

Well...there you have it, thought I. He's drawn his line in the sand. He likes me, just not in *that* way. Whatever. I was so over Bruces anyway.

He took me home, and I thought the date was over. I was mistaken (first time ever).

"What shall we do now, Miss Vickie?" he queried as we pulled into my driveway.

Do? I thought we were just friends? We're not going to *do* anything.

"Well, I don't know Bruce. What did you want to do?"

"I'd like to come in and hear you sing a song." No hesitation at all. That's what he wanted.

My gut told me there was no danger in this plan so I played piano and sang an original song. He asked for an encore. I obliged. He still didn't leave so I poured myself a glass of wine while he drank water. My dog mauled him on the sofa while I sat innocently across the room, observing the spectacle.

"I'm not really a dog person," he admitted, in between petting Shiloh and getting licked in return. Oh really? Except there he was, calmly sitting on a leather couch while a rambunctious and goofy golden doodle either pawed him incessantly or rolled over onto his back begging for a belly rub. Bruce didn't ask me to call off the dog. He didn't run for the door. He just sat there playing with my dog as if he was in fact a dog person.

I really didn't know what to make of this guy, but I was leaving the next day for a weekend in Nashville with my dear old friend, Tina, so making another date didn't seem urgent. And to be truthful (as opposed to all the other times I've lied to you) I wasn't even sure I wanted another date with Bruce. Do the math. It wasn't adding up. I knew that we looked good together. Quite frankly the guy would look good with Phyllis Diller. I just didn't know if we'd *be* good together.

He kissed me lightly on the lips. "I'd like you to call me when you get back, Vickie. I'd really like to see you again." He kissed me again. "I know you may not believe it but I really am a touchy-feely kind of guy."

Yeah, right. He had been nice enough and cute enough but I wouldn't exactly describe him as warm. Well, except with the dog.

He kissed me again. The earth did not move. I gave him my CD. It's just a little live thing I had thrown together to sell in the clubs, with a few originals tossed into the mix. He seemed so interested in my music so *here's a lovely parting gift, selected especially for you!* I figured he'd enjoy it. He thanked me and left. A minute later he came back because he had forgotten his phone. This time I kissed him. I was waiting for that damn earth to move. I wanted the damn earth to move.

Still nothing. Not even an itsy bitsy tremor.

Oh well, thought I as I drifted off to sleep. No need to even think about this one for now. I could deal with Bruce #3 after my trip. Or never.

So, there I was in Nashville having dinner (augmented by meat and lots of wine) with Tina and two of her male friends and I put the question to the table: "Can a wine-loving carnivore ever forge a successful relationship with a teetotaling vegetarian?" The answer was an immediate and resounding NO! The jury had spoken.

The next day Bruce sent me this email:

> *Do you give your CD to all your dates or just the ones that might be in for a return engagement? Or am I a special case? I love your CD. I have it in my pick-up. I was on my way to my boat to do some winterizing; playing your CD. I never made it. I turned around and came back here to fire off this email. I particularly liked* Crazy. *Then I heard* I Wanna Come Home to You. *It sounded like you were singing it to me. "I want to live by the water." I got this odd feeling. You probably get this all the time.*

Here's a confession. I get that, like, never.

Crazy is the Patsy Cline standard. *I Wanna Come Home to You* is an original and, if I had to pick one song that sums up me and my life-relationship goal, this would be it. All about not needing anything fancy, just needing that one special person to come home to. He said it *sounded like I was singing to him.* He got *an odd feeling.* Wow. I was tingling all over as I stared at the email. I read it to myself several times and then I read it aloud to Tina. My feelings for Captain Bruce had suddenly taken a huge turn. As a matter of fact, as I sat there at Tina's dining room table in Nashville re-reading these words from a man I barely knew a thousand miles away, I think the damn earth finally moved.

Guess what happened? Oh, never mind. I'll tell you.

Captain Bruce became my boyfriend! And it was good. As a matter of fact, at the beginning it was very good. We started dating right before Christmas and I can honestly say Christmas that year was one of my best ever. Loads of romance and magic. With a man who doesn't drink or eat meat. Who'da thunk it? I still enjoyed my morning latte, I still drank wine and I never had to be the designated driver (woo hoo!). Bruce actually said to me early on in our relationship, "I don't care if you have a glass of wine in your hand 24/7."

Brilliant!

And he liked my son. A lot. Well really — who wouldn't? Jack liked him too. My dog adored him (in a slobbery dog kinda way). My friends liked him (mostly they liked how he made me feel), a few of them referred to him as the "hot guy" and my family welcomed him graciously. I had fallen in love with a man who never would have appeared to be the man of my dreams. Which led me to this astonishing conclusion: better to fall in love when you're awake. More on that in a minute but now let's get to that tofu. Because vegetables, fruit, pasta, eggs and cheese were not enough for Bruce. He needed protein and Bruce loves tofu. And since I loved Bruce I decided to learn to love tofu.

The first thing that every good cheater will learn about tofu is this: if you buy the plain old regular kind it will taste like, well, a sponge. They say that tofu is like shrimp and it will take on the characteristics of whatever you marinate it in. I must have been marinating all my plain old regular tofu in sponge because that's what it tasted like. Then I discovered pre-flavoured tofu. Who knew? Tofu that someone else has marinated! Whatever magic dust they sprinkled on it worked because pre-flavoured tofu tastes like whatever it was pre-flavoured to taste like. I tried teriyaki, coconut curry and herb and they all taste considerably more flavourful than any sponge I ever attempted to flavour. So go ahead — cheat! Let someone else do the work.

Speaking of **Coconut Curry,** here's the recipe:

> **1 package coconut curry tofu,** cubed
>
> **1 jar coconut curry sauce mix** Yes, you can actually buy it pre-coconutted. In a jar. If you're making lots use 2 jars, or just add a can of regular yellow curry sauce
>
> **Whatever fabulous vegetables your adventuresome heart desires,** chopped to bite-size pieces. I love bok choy, broccoli, carrots, sweet onion but also think peppers (any colour), mushrooms or cauliflower

The trick is to fry up the tofu first. Throw it into a dollop of butter before you do anything else. Make it nice and crispy. Some restaurants even deep-fry, but I don't own one of those wonderful contraptions because I'd be eating French fries all the time. So just fry it up. I suppose if you were super health conscience (like Bruce, whose fabulous lips had not touched butter for many years before he met me), you'd use olive oil. Alas, I am taste conscious more than health conscious, and I just use a teensy dollop. Just enough to grease the bottom of a non-stick pan, which means not very much at all.

Transfer the tofu to a pot and add everything else. Simmer away till you're too curious to wait another moment, serve over rice and there you have it — a sweet, spicy meatless meal that you could almost cook blindfolded.

Teriyaki Tofu with Mushrooms

> **1 package teriyaki tofu,** chopped into bite-size pieces
>
> **2 cups cremini (or whatever you like) mushrooms,** sliced
>
> **fresh spinach**
>
> **1/2 cup goat cheese**

I'm pretty sure you know me so well by now that you could whip this up in a heartbeat without my instructions. Fry up the tofu in butter. Set aside. Fry up the mushrooms in a tad more butter. You can add some fresh ground pepper here but I'd probably stay away from the Montreal steak spice — it's too strong a flavour and will conflict with the teriyaki. Reintroduce (is that a legit cooking term?) the tofu to the mushrooms, toss in a whole bunch of fresh spinach and when it's almost wilted to perfection, add the goat cheese. If I wasn't cooking for Bruce I'd probably toss in some white wine just to make it a little saucy. I've learned that vegetable broth will almost always do the trick. Simmer it all for a few minutes and then serve with a warm baguette or over pasta or rice.

Herbed Tofu with Cilantro and Black Olives

I invented this dish on a solo evening (yes, I still had them despite the boyfriend thing) when I was yet again emptying out my fridge. I first made it with Cajun chicken, available pre-spiced and ready, but then used herbed tofu for Bruce. Both turned out great.

---

1 package herbed tofu (or 2 Cajun chicken breasts), chopped into bite-size pieces

1 large tomato, diced

1 cup cilantro, chopped

fresh ground pepper

1/2 cup pre-seasoned feta cheese (there are many different kinds), crumbled

whole bunch fresh spinach

1/2 cup vegetable stock or wine

As above, my friend, as above! Fry up the tofu (or meat), add all the other ingredients, simmer till it's hot and serve over pasta. And here's my new favourite healthy trick: you know I love spinach. You also know that once it's cooked and wilted it pretty much doesn't even exist anymore (except for some yummy flavour) so I serve all my pasta dishes on a bed of fresh spinach. Yes, even more spinach! Simply half-fill the individual pasta dishes with fresh spinach. Dump on your pasta and top with whatever delectable delight you just created. You don't even need to make a salad. It's a one-plate meal, perfect for watching movies or sitting on the deck on a warm summer night.

I confess I never ventured into dessert tofu. I couldn't really see the point. Bruce hadn't sworn off dairy or sugar or flour or chocolate so there were plenty of "real" desserts available to him. But the other kind of tofu I enjoyed was the simulated ground beef. It also comes pre-flavoured: Mexican (perfect for tacos), Italian (spaghetti) and Asian (stir fry). Very tasty and — honestly — I didn't miss ground beef at all. Okay, that's a lie. One night I made tacos for Bruce and Jack so we had real and fake meat. I ate the real meat, but I could see myself eventually eating less and less of it. This vegetarian stuff is not half bad.

What ultimately happened with the good Captain and me? We had a few really lovely months and then we began to struggle. There were times we just didn't click. And then times we did. And then not. Back and forth like a see-saw we went. When his father died ten months after we started dating, we grew very close. We even bought a house together. I had decided that when Jack was done high school I wanted to live somewhere near water. Southampton was prohibitively expensive and, as much as I love Vancouver, my job, my family and my friends were all in Ontario. My cousin and her husband had recently relocated to a charming town called Meaford on the shores of Georgian Bay. And so Bruce, Jack and I visited once I had done a little real estate research that showed Meaford prices were ridiculously, wonderfully low. I even found a house I loved. An old red brick beauty that had been reconstructed to include a huge great room at the back, perfect for my baby grand, Bruce's drums and a pool table!

Jack was off to Los Angeles that fall to start music college and I was ready for this new adventure. Ready for small town living. Ready for a cool old house. Ready for walks by the water and outdoor fires and semi-retirement. Bruce said he was ready for a new life too. I'm just not sure he actually meant it. We bought the house. We knew it needed a ton of work but hey, Bruce is a carpenter after all, and the plan was he would eventually quit the movie business in Toronto and start up his own renovation business in Meaford.

Well, long story longer (is there any other way with me?), things didn't quite work out as planned (do they ever?). I sold my house in Guelph, moved to my sweet little northern town, found myself a cute young contractor who looked like Brad Pitt (hey, I needed to have sixteen new doors hung and he came highly recommended) and I began the business of turning our fixer-upper into a fixed-up jewel. Dylan (aka Brad) came over almost every night after his day job and by and by the place was looking good. New flooring, new bathroom, new kitchen, new doors — pretty much new everything. Since I didn't have a lot of new friends yet, Dylan's company was most welcome, and he gave me someone to cook for almost every night. I was grateful for more than one reason.

Bruce came to the house every weekend and occasionally lay some baseboards or hung a light, but for the most part he really was not interested in working on our house after working all week on sets. This made me a bit crazy. After all, it was *our* house, and he was the one with the skills. Luckily, I was the one with some cash and zero patience so the renovations (with Dylan) continued.

But Bruce and I struggled with different approaches toward finances. We struggled with interior decorating concepts. We struggled with communication. We never struggled with booze or meat (I did my thing, he did his) but we did struggle with the concept of happiness. You see, my dear Bruce believed that in a good relationship people are just happy. Period. No work, no effort, no conscious design. They just are.

I beg to differ.

Shortly before my marriage tanked, my fabulous husband and I engaged in a heart-to-heart I remember well. We were hiding in our bedroom whilst our pals and kids mingled in the living room of our Quebec rental chalet. We were on a group holiday and I wasn't having very much fun. Wasn't quite sure why. The skiing was fine. I just knew I was running on empty and needed something to keep our union from imploding. And this was before Grover. So, we had the "heart talk." We didn't do this often. Probably because my heart was always in secret turmoil and HBS's heart was typically resigned and quiet. But on this auspicious occasion he uttered something so beautifully profound it has stuck with me these many years since. Those words? "I only want to do three things in this life. I want to take care of you and our son, I want to build machinery, and I want to make music. Whatever else it is that you need, I'm not sure I can do." Turns out he was right because I had no clue what I needed. I just knew I needed more.

By the time I got to Bruce I knew you had to actually "do" things to achieve happiness. So, one night when we were speeding along a major highway I put the question to him.

"Bruce, tell me three things you want to do in this life. Just three important goals."

He was none too excited about this query but finally muttered through frustrated lips, "I just want to be happy."

Oh. Golly. Never thought of that. I mean seriously? We all just wanna be happy. The question is — what are you going to do to get happy? He seemed to think that serene happiness was his God-given right, thank you very much, and that it would just magically float down from heaven and land on his head. Even when I persisted and offered once more, "I understand that Bruce, but what do you want to *do* to create that happiness?"

He had no answers.

In hindsight, I think I probably could have answered for him: Motorcycles, Freedom, Music. The boy loves motorcycles. Buying them. Riding them (he used to race until he suffered a horrific crash). Tinkering with them. Buying more of them. Talking with other riders about them. That was his passion.

Freedom. And by that I mean freedom from the constraints of "normal" society. He didn't want a mortgage or a white picket fence. He was happy living on a tiny sailboat or in a basement apartment. He worked when he could or when he needed to but loved the freedom to just turn down a job (or not apply for one) and travel in his VW bus or on his bike.

Music. Bruce was an aspiring drummer and he loved to make and listen to music (even me).

The dilemma was that we only shared the music passion. I love to travel but I also love my home and having space for my baby grand. Motorcycles? Just not my thing. Neither is camping in a VW bus for weeks or months on end. Earlier, I said these pursuits seemed adventuresome to me, but the reality was a different story. Sitting behind Bruce on his "crotch rocket" hurt my back and neck. And the thought of camping in his semi-renovated VW bus and sleeping on an ancient sagging mattress hurt my back and neck even more.

Finally, after putting off Bruce's move-in date more than once (I was surprisingly happy with the part-time arrangement) and after a few too many struggles, and after I spent two weeks in LA with my son where I gained immense clarity, and after one too many painful dust-ups, I ended it. The bathtub was already empty, I just pulled the plug. We were both unhappy more often than not, and the struggles had become too intense. I knew it had to end. I knew I had to be free to find something (someone) different. I knew he did too.

So that was the end of Bruce #3. We sold our perfectly renovated home, Bruce moved back to the big city (he never had given up his apartment) and I bought a very cute smaller house that had just been gutted and renovated (by someone else, thank goodness, because I wasn't ready for that again). Interestingly, one evening Bruce came up to Meaford to pick up some stuff and we went out for dinner. We were very cordial, civil, even loving. As I sipped my first mouthful of Pinot Grigio I must have sighed or something because he said, "You know, Vickie, you really need to be with someone who enjoys food and drink as much as you do." He was right. Creating food, drinking wine, candlelight, music — these are all things I hold very dear to my heart. Being with a man who by his own admission only "eats for fuel" and would never enjoy that first cold sip of wine was not optimal.

And so, I went back online. What else can a girl do?

Hopeless (Helpless) Romantics

PARDON ME WHILE I DIGRESS YET AGAIN. Only because I really want to include this kid-friendly recipe and tell you a little story that goes with it. I'll try to be brief (yeah, right).

One of my oldest friends (and I don't mean *old* old, I just mean I've known her since high school) is Darlene. We were best buds at eighteen, drifted apart, came back together for her wedding (she was a very young bride) and then had some ridiculous tiff that kept us apart for over twenty-five years. I certainly thought about her a lot over the decades. She lives virtually in my sister's back yard. I don't mean in a tent or anything, I mean her back yard pretty much abuts my sister's back yard. I just never found the gumption to ring her bell and say, "Hey, what's up?"

Then our high school threw a huge reunion. Just prior I was having lunch with another old buddy, Peter F. Truth be told Peter F wasn't just an old buddy. He was the boy I was madly (and secretly) in love with from Grade 4 to Grade 6 and again all through high school. We had a two-year break (Grades 7 and 8) when we went to different schools. You know, out of sight, out of mind. At the end of Grade 10, I had a party in my basement and Peter F, who had barely ever even spoken to me, danced with me slow and then HOLY SHIT we shared a few passionate kisses. I thought *Heaven has finally arrived!*

Nope. Turns out those were his very first kisses ever (I wasn't far ahead) and I was told by a mutual pal that something spooked him. That was it. There was no further contact with my long-time crush for the rest of that school year. By the start of Grade 11 he had a girlfriend — you know, one who wasn't me. Apparently, he wasn't that spooked. Bastard. I was completely devastated in that get-over-it-real-quick teenage kinda way.

Peter F and I had very little contact throughout the rest of high school but after university I would bump into him somewhere every few years. At a mall, at the bank, in a restaurant, once at a New Year's gala where I was performing; I was always bumping into Peter F. It was initially him with an assortment of girls and, ultimately, with the beautiful Gina who became his wife. We ended up living in the same city (not our hometown but close) and finally, after about twenty-five years, I invited him and his family to dine with me and mine. I was still married and Jack was probably nine.

It was a fun evening. Gina was well aware of the fact that I was her hubby's first kiss (a tiny little thing I had for some reason neglected to mention to my husband). I had invited another couple (mostly to remind me of who I had become, not who I *was*) and we all made merry. I even made a bit of music, much to the delight of Peter's two young daughters. It was a grand time, but I will admit I was completely transported back to high school insecurities. I mean for crying out loud this was Peter F! Star of my schoolgirl dreams! The one that got away. Yes, I was no longer the confident, comfy-in-my-skin broad I thought I had become. I was the jilted crush, destined to forever wonder why I wasn't good enough for Peter F.

The next day he and I exchanged a few emails, starting with the standard thank-you and moving on to harmless chat. I finally thought: what the hell? I'm not some giggling schoolgirl anymore. I am a woman of talent and accomplishment and I will no longer cower in the shadows of some guy who rebuked my undying love not only in high school but grade school as well! I am WOMAN, hear me roar. I will not be held hostage by this unrequited love a moment longer! I can take ownership of this relationship! In the next email I asked him, *What happened? Why those big kisses in Grade 10 and then nothing? Was I not pretty enough? Not popular enough? Unlikely to put out (I was a late bloomer)? What was it?*

He was understandably astonished by my candour, flattered I'm sure and eager to explain. As far as he could see, I was the smart girl. The girl doing musicals, on student council, getting top grades. He was the "stoner" boy, partying his way through school, not really accomplishing much of anything except getting high and having fun. He didn't think I could possibly be into him! We had nothing in common.

Boys are stupid.

Anyway, he invited me to lunch, and I realized I am so over Peter F. I mean, I already knew I was over him. I quickly discovered I was over the insecurities he had inspired for oh-so many years. It's funny how you can hang on to an unrequited crush long after you've morphed into an entirely new and improved human being. I'm pretty sure it's all about that word "unrequited." Because if Peter F and I had dated in high school, it probably would have lasted about a minute. He's a really sweet and also cool guy who totally pulled it together after graduating. He cleaned up his act, went on to get not only one but two degrees and is currently teaching at the university level. I am so proud of him I could write a sonnet and he is still most definitely not the guy for me. Still damn cute I will tell you, but not the guy for me. I guess he was right all along! Regardless, at that lunch (we've had many since) we were talking about the upcoming reunion and he said, "Who would you like to reconnect with most?" Without skipping a beat I replied "Darlene." I didn't know if she would be there or how it would be if we met after all these years. I just knew she was the one person I desperately wanted to see.

About three weeks before the reunion I received an email via my radio station's website. The subject: *Hey Buku*. I'm Buku. My sister studied in Russia, and when she returned with all that new-found knowledge (put the vodka in the freezer!) she showed me that in the Russian alphabet, my name looks like Buku. Everyone called me Buku for a time but with Darlene it really stuck. She even signed my yearbook to Buku! So when I saw that email, I knew immediately that it was from her. I couldn't believe it. She asked me if I remembered her. Huh? How could I possibly forget? That girl and I got into more underage drinking, smoking, older guy trouble than should be legal. Oh wait — it wasn't. Boy, did we have fun! Turns out she had been at a party (in our hometown where she still lives) and she overheard my name in a conversation. Well, almost my name. See, my legal maiden name is Dyck. Pronounced Dyke. I specify that because in Waterloo, where I grew up, a lot of people pronounce that Dick. But no, we were Dycks. Except my mother was actually a Dick (pronounced Dick) before she became a Dyck (pronounced Dyke). I am so not kidding and I think you can probably surmise now why I changed my professional name to van Dyke. So, there's Darlene at this party listening to some stranger talk about Vickie van Dyke who just may be the Vickie Dyck from high school and she butts in and says *Huh?* And she finds out that I sing regularly at this little bistro (where these people had seen me) and I'm a DJ at some jazz station in Hamilton. Well, resourceful girl that she is, Darlene Googles, finds me and emails. All this less than two weeks after my lunch with Peter F. Talk about destiny!

A few days later she and her husband and some friends showed up at that restaurant where I sang and somehow they were miraculously seated right in front of the band. We had already started our first set when they arrived so we didn't have a chance to talk or hug, but at the end of that set I dedicated a song to her (*If* by Bread) and we were both bawling like babies. We ended up going to the reunion together and in no time at all were right back to where we left off, thick as aging thieves. Not that we ever actually steal anything. But she was a rep for General Mills and, much to the delight of my son, often brought free samples to our house. And this is where we (finally!) get to the recipe.

I'm getting worse, aren't I?

The thing is, General Mills makes Hamburger Helper, which Jack loved. It truly is the ultimate cheat but I rarely bought it because it's just too boring to cook. Where's the fun for me? So, one night as a special treat for Jack I created a homemade version.

Hamburger Helpless

---

1 lb. lean ground beef

1 small can tomato or spaghetti sauce

1 cup Cheese Whiz (melted) or Queso Mexican sauce (if you like that jalapeno kick)

1 small onion, chopped

2 tsp. garlic

whole bunch fresh ground pepper

other spices to taste (basil, oregano, cayenne if you want some kick)

1 box whole wheat elbow macaroni

1/2 cup asiago, Parmesan, mozzarella (or a mixture of all of them!), grated

---

Brown the beef with the onion. At the same time, boil the macaroni according to the package instructions. Strain the grease from the beef and add the tomato sauce, melted Cheese Whiz or Queso and spices. At this point, feel free to toss in whatever old vegetables you have lying around. I used frozen green beans but corn, peas, carrots or celery would all work well too. Add the cooked macaroni and stir. Transfer the entire concoction to a casserole dish and top with grated cheese. Bake at 350F for 30 minutes and then broil for a few minutes at the end to brown up the cheese. You could even add breadcrumbs to the top if you want some crunch. Or maybe even dried/fried onions.

And there you have it — the ultimate kid-friendly one-pot meal! Jack's first bite comment? "Mom, you're gonna have to make this again."

Peter F and I are still friends. And Darlene and I shall never again part, guaranteed.

And Then Came Robert...

LIVING IN THE THRIVING UN-METROPOLIS OF MEAFORD AND GOING BACK TO THE ONLINE DATING WORLD WAS A REAL EYE-OPENER. Turns out geography plays a big part in the dating numbers game and if you're a two-hour drive from Toronto or any other thriving southern Ontario metropolis, chances are men in those cities won't be willing to make the trek. Toronto to Guelph? No problem. Toronto to Meaford (where the hell is that)? No thanks, sister.

That's not to say that the pickings were sumptuous anywhere. In my five years of shopping for a guy online I discovered that the older one gets, the less one has to choose from. That would be if one hopes to find someone in one's age group or at least one's generation. The thing is, after fifty you find out that most of the "good ones" are already partnered. It is a hard, messy slog wading through the rest of that lot. Still, I was there and (I'd like to believe) still worthy. And I only wanted one. Didn't need a buffet. Just one perfectly imperfect mate. I believed with all my heart he could be there too. He sure wasn't strolling the streets of Meaford, bellowing my name.

Because I am so picky (unlike Grover who, if Jack's word could be trusted, was working on his sixth or seventh post-Vickie relationship at that time), I was fully expecting another long drought of romantic interaction. After Grover left me (for the fourth time, which I repeat constantly because most of my girlfriends find it hilarious), I went over six months until Charlie came around. After Charlie, another six months until Ben. After Ben (who wasn't really a relationship, just ask him) a measly three months until Billy. And after Billy it took eight months for Bruce #3 to show up. I was prepared for the long haul.

And so I walked the dog, started writing a blog, made new friends in Meaford, did some gigs and walked the dog some more. I was no longer working on radio so I filled my days with charitable endeavours, cooking for friends and walking the dog. And when I walked the dog I would dialogue with the Universe daily and ask, "Please just bring me one last love of my life. Please and thank you."

I was two months into renewed single-hood and even though I had struck up a few conversations and correspondences, nobody was exactly jumping off the screen. It was a lonely time. I didn't have Jack anymore. He was back from LA but living with his dad "down south." I didn't have Dylan anymore (renovations were done and he had a new girlfriend), I didn't have a job to go to once a week or a man to cook for. I had a dog and online dating.

And then came Robert. As all those faces scrolled past me daily (and believe me, you get to know them quickly) his literally jumped off the screen — he is just that damn cute. So, I checked out his profile. First off, he had lots of pictures posted, something I believe to be an irrefutable necessity when online dating. I mean come on, we all have at least one really good picture, and we can all Photoshop at least one really good picture, but the number of times I have been aghast with incredulity when faced with the reality, well, too numerous to mention. My theory is a man who posts lots of photos has nothing to hide, and that was Robert. A cute head shot (with a full head of thick, dark hair). A cute sitting shot (in jeans and a denim shirt). A cute standing shot (in suit and tie). And then pics of him scuba diving, ice climbing and mountaineering. Damn! And I know — what the heck is up with me and mountain climbers? So, I read his profile (well-written, no glaring grammatical errors, which is always a turn-off for me) and checked out his stats. He was a scientist! He had a master's degree. I come from a family of educators so this was big news. He worked at a university (even better!). He was single with no children and he liked dogs. Brilliant.

And then came the bad news. He lived in Hamilton, a 2.5-hour drive away. I knew this because that is where my radio station was and that was the reason I no longer worked there. The other disconcerting news was Robert is eight years younger than I. Now don't get me wrong. I take no issue with younger men. Indeed, my ex-husband, Grover, Charlie, Ben, Bruce #3 are all younger than I. But by a few months to a couple of years. Not eight! *Yikes*! thought I sadly. *There is no way this guy is going to be interested in an old bag like me. Especially an old bag such a lengthy drive away.*

However, never one to let fear or logic stand in the way of potential love, I sent him a brief note: "You're damn cute." That's all it said. I had learned many missives ago that your first effort should be short and sweet, funny and/or intriguing. Off it went into the ether and I waited. Thankfully it didn't take Robert long to respond. He was just a tad wordier than I had been, penning something like "Well, insomuch as a man of my age can be labeled as cute I appreciate the sentiment even whilst doubting its actual veracity." Like I said, something like that. And so it began. We went back and forth numerous times (within the confines of the dating site) sharing snippets of our lives, hobbies, interests and his work (marine biology). I found out he actually holds a PhD, not just a master's, a fact that piqued my interest even further. Our written chats were interesting and engaging, but he never flirted. Not even once and not even vaguely. It was all very friendly and I eventually thought, *Okay, this guy just wants me to be his friend, nothing more. Fair enough.* Until he mentioned that if I ever did another gig "down south" he would come and watch me perform. As it turns out I did have a gig on the books, very much in his neighbourhood, so I replied, "If we actually do meet in person do you think we would have anything to talk about? After all, you are a scientist and I am a musician." His response (and these were his exact words): "I look upon this as an opportunity to test the hypothesis that opposites attract."

BAM! He had me. Robert was flirting!

We moved from the dating site to regular email and from email to our first phone call, all in one day. I had already learned that he was British (with ten years in Canada under his belt) but I sure as heck wasn't prepared for the accent when he first called. HBS comes from British stock and his parents still live in England so I had spent a lot of time across the pond. But Robert's accent is "West Country" and a language unto itself. I actually had difficulty understanding him at times. At other times, I was completely taken with the unusual cadence (he often gets mistaken for an Australian). That first call lasted well over two hours. By its end we had established he would visit me in

Meaford on the upcoming weekend, which happened to be a long one and the first official weekend of summer (May 24). This man was in no way put off by the lengthy commute. He told me he was looking forward to it. A lovely drive in the country? What's not to like?

The next night's phone call commenced at midnight and lasted well into the wee hours. We had been texting all day and he told me he had a conference call lined up for a potential job in New Zealand and wasn't sure when it would begin or wrap up. I said, "Just call me when you're done. Doesn't matter when. I can sleep in tomorrow." And so he did. The next evening and the one after that as well. By the time he finally showed up on the Saturday of the long weekend we had logged over ten hours in phone time, augmented by many emails and texts. We knew each other!

Yeah, right. Famous last words (again). Can opposites really attract and then hold? I mean for more than just a night and a quick hop in the hay? Veteran soul-searcher that I am, I looked back on all my loves and I thought — hmmm, what actually works best? Lots of commonalities or lots of differences? Might opposites truly click or are we best to stick with our own kind? How the fuck should I know? I've tried it both ways and both worked on some levels and both didn't work on some levels. I've been soul-mated with another fragile, tortured poet and I've been married to a practical, get-it-done provider. I've shared tofu with a non-drinking vegetarian and I've gnawed on bones with a wine-swilling drunk. I've contemplated a gypsy existence with Peter Pan and I've lived the Pepsi commercial life with the "greatest guy on earth." And I still had no idea what I wanted or needed. Do you think this was possibly due to the fact that I still had no idea who I was? Some of my girlfriends thought so. They counselled me to spend time alone and learn to love myself.

Fine. Except (all humility aside) I already thought I was all that and a bag of chips. I mean really, there in my middle-aged dotage, exactly how much alone time did I need? Shiloh and I were getting bored. So, countered I, maybe I know exactly who I am and who I am is a combination of all of the above and if Prince Charming would just flipping well show up and be all those things, I could finally throw away all my other shoes and just wear that fucking glass slipper. Okay. We all know that wasn't gonna happen. First of all, I'm too old for a prince and secondly I'm clumsy. Wine glasses don't ever stand a chance in my house. What are the odds a glass slipper would survive?

So, there was Robert in the flesh. Ridiculously intelligent, accomplished, communicative, youthful, a whole lot more inside-the-box (except for when he wasn't) and a little emotionally unavailable. Okay, maybe a lot emotionally unavailable. I wasn't sure yet but there were red flags reminding me of dear old British HBS. We were not immediately and effortlessly simpatico. We had a unique connection, as evidenced by those marathon phone conversations. We were fully capable of engaging intellectually and physically. Our first kiss, instigated by him, thank you very much, happened right after we'd finished lunch (homemade pizza) and were sipping wine at my kitchen counter. Yes, Robert liked wine. And beer. And Scotch. And rum. And meat. I could listen to him talk about his work endlessly and find it fascinating. This is where I should admit that his work is highly left brain and I pretty much lost contact with my left brain around Grade 10 when I decided that dissecting a frog could in no way factor into my quest to become the next Carole King. And yet when he spoke, I listened. And sometimes I even asked questions, which he was delighted to answer, mercifully without a hint of patronization. Damnit if that boy had ever patronized me even for a second I swear I would have hit him over the head with my baby grand.

He was also able, somewhat shyly, to veer off his own straight-and-narrow to ask me a question or two about my music and writing. And he actually seemed interested in my response, in that "Holy Crap, you really are from another planet" kind of way.

Turns out we could also engage physically (much later, honest) because, well, I'm not really sure why. Just because we did. And it worked.

What scared me from Day 2 was that elusive emotional availability. It was already pretty clear to me that we were at opposite ends of the emotion spectrum. Me the open book, heart-on-my-sleeve girl. I couldn't play it any other way, nor did I want to. Robert was decidedly more reserved, restrained and closed off. He wouldn't even hold my hand in public. I was wondering, how much room is there for evolution? Could people really change? (I fully require a public hand-holder.)

So, back to my original question: can opposites really attract? Because as has been so eloquently stated: *A fish may love a bird, but where would they live?* I thought *Oh what the hell?* I had taken stupider chances in my life. I decided I was willing to embrace what made us different, revel in what made us fit, enjoy what made us unique and look forward to what might eventually make us...us. I abandoned preconceived notions of what works and what doesn't and just made every effort to enjoy the ride. And if "opposites attracting" was just some lame fodder for chick-flicks, so be it. Lesson learned and off we could ride into opposite sunsets.

Okay I know, I know. Even this right-brained dope knows there can be no such thing as opposite sunsets. But, if the desire to be attracted and open, and to delight in discovery and the new and the different... if that desire could potentially propel us to a new level of honest relationship (you know, boldly go where no man has gone before!) well, the struggle would be worth it. And opposites just might not be so opposite after all.

So, we soldiered on. I visited him at his home in Hamilton and he returned to Meaford many times. I moved into my new house and he helped every step of the way. Shiloh fell madly in love with him and Robert fell madly in love with Shiloh and Meaford. I could feel myself falling but we both steered clear of those three magic words as if uttering them might undo all the positive strides we had taken.

And then it hit me. And it hit me hard. Robert was an "I" guy. Not a "we" guy. And I most definitely was looking for a "we" guy. When we're young (like say, back in our 40s), we don't really know what we want. So we allow chemistry to rule and libidos to lead. I'll admit that even now my libido often lobbies for front rank, but at that time I had established a few other non-negotiables that I tried to check in with regularly. Things I absolutely needed in a relationship with a man.

– Emotional intimacy. I needed to know that my man and I could talk. About everything/anything. I needed to see my man's heart and show mine freely with an absence of fear.

Robert would listen to me talk for hours and nod his head at the right times but there was a lack of deep, emotional sharing from him. Even when he relayed stories of past loves they were quick and dry. He was incredible at talking, just not emotional sharing.

– Connectedness. No matter where we were or what we were doing I needed to know that I still figured prominently in his life. A quick phone call, a few texts, the odd email — I needed to stay connected.

Robert went away on business for days or weeks on end and pretty much forgot I existed. I might get a text every three or four days or he might answer the phone if I called, but his communication skills were sorely lacking. He told me this was because he compartmentalizes. When he is working, he thinks work. When he was with me he could think about me.

– Emotional maturity. Yes I am a free spirit and yes I'm a bit of a gypsy and yes I could pack up and move every year and yes I'd be happy vagabonding the world — but — I am a grown-up. I pay my bills on time, keep my home reasonably clean, try not to speed too often, and live within my means. I am responsible. Enough. I required a man who was the same.

Thankfully Robert earned full marks on this count. He too was a grown-up.

– Spark. Yep, it has to be there or all the "on paper" qualities wouldn't add up to a hill of baked beans.

And yes, thankfully Robert and I had plenty of spark.

– Intellectual compatibility. My man needs to be able to teach me some stuff. Stuff I actually want to learn. And I need to teach him stuff too. The role of full-time teacher doesn't appeal to me at all, nor does that of full-time student. And I don't want to be anybody's mama. I already have a kid, thank you very much.

Yes, we were also aces in this department, no complaints.

What scared me is that I had realized it was the "I" guys who were still on the market. My guess is because most "I" guys either A) don't want to compromise, evolve or commit to a "We" relationship or B) they just don't know how. They haven't learned the tools, they haven't had enough practice and now all they feel comfortable with is tending to the "I." Factoring in another "I" and therefore creating a "We" is foreign territory, uncomfortable and terrifying. Not to mention work. You never have to work on being an "I" because guess what? You already are. Being a "We" takes work. Conscious effort. Desire. And then more work.

So what exactly differentiates a "We" guy from an "I" guy? Allow me to get scientific just for a moment:

	"We" Guy	"I" Guy
Got your back	A "We" guy has your back. Your emotional back. He pays attention to the signals, is available when you need to talk, not only offers to listen but really listens and then offers sensitive, supportive advice. It's even okay if having your back is a tad inconvenient for him. Your back is important to him and he shows it.	An "I" guy has your back (or so he thinks). But his idea of having your back is being there to chop down a tree or two, put gas in your lawn mower or fix your computer. As long as he can be manly, show off a bit and hopefully operate a power tool or two, he's definitely got your back, baby.

Understanding	A "We" guy understands that you are an emotional girl and sometimes just need to cry. He acknowledges that it doesn't always make sense. Maybe it's just a build up of saltwater? Maybe you're a certifiable nut? He doesn't care. He holds you, offers tissues, tells you you're beautiful even with mascara streaming down your cheeks, and just lets you cry.	An "I" guy freaks out. He assumes it's all about him (because everything is), goes on the defensive, reminds you that he did nothing wrong and turns away when you blow your nose because he can't stand the thought of snot escaping from your chapped nostrils.
The Prize	A "We" guy acknowledges that the sum of the relationship's parts is more important than individual desires. The goal is to be together. To be contentedly partnered. To have each other's backs for all time. From this he extrapolates that compromise is always required. So nothing — ever — is cast in stone. Everything is up for discussion and negotiable (except the non-negotiables, of course) because his eye is always on the prize. And the prize is partnership.	An "I" guy wants what he wants when he wants it, how he wants it, where he wants it, and if you can support all his wants and then somehow fit your ass into his scenario, he's okay with having you around. But if you question his wants, if you question how his wants and yours might ultimately mesh, if you question the fact that his wants always take precedence over yours, the "I" guy will run for the hills. And then blame you for chasing him away and/or the demise of the relationship. Because hell, girl, you were too needy!

Connection	A "We" guy stays connected because you are the most important person in his life and he wants you to know it. He genuinely cares about your day, your work, your passions, your life. And so he checks in regularly from wherever he is in the world. He feeds your partnership with words and questions and caring and presence. He is present in your relationship even when he is a million miles away.	An "I" guy is busy. Busy doing his thing, his work, his hobbies, his life. So, sometimes (too many times) he forgets to check in. It's mostly because when he isn't with you — guess what? — he isn't with you. And you are not with him. Don't worry, he'll get back to you when he needs another fix of you, but he is a lone wolf, this "I" guy. He runs in a pack of one. And when he catches any kind of scent that gets his tail a-wagging, you no longer exist until he's back in his lair, cold and lonely. Then he will connect with you. Because when his solo adventure is over, then he needs you. He needs you to fulfill his needs.

Robert was willing to listen to me blab and wipe my tears, but the rest of him was leaning precariously into "I" guy territory. He was, after all, a forty-eight-year-old man who had never even lived with a woman full-time, much less committed to a partnership. He was used to being a lone wolf; that was all he knew.

So I asked him THE question. What are the three things you want to do with your life?

And he replied:

1) I want to be recognized in my field. Do great work and have it acknowledged by my peers.

2) There are a few more mountains I'd like to climb. (Just in case you think he's being poetic I can assure you he means this quite literally. As I mentioned, he is a mountaineer and has even threatened to drag my old ass up a slope or two.)

3) I'd like to have someone to share it all with.

I loved his answer and I loved those three things. I loved that he had ambition and drive (and the intelligence to back it up), I loved that he was athletic and physical and — dare I say — daring. And I loved that for him being in a relationship made the first two even better. I wasn't about to suddenly invest in a petri dish or bag Everest, but I knew I could be there with champagne and hugs when he wins the Nobel and returns from the climb with a grin on his face (all in one piece, thank you very much).

Robert and I discussed this whole I/We thing and he acknowledged that he wanted to be a "we" guy but perhaps didn't have the necessary tools — yet. We decided to work on it.

Then came our first Christmas together. He was taking his annual pilgrimage back to Merry Olde to visit his father and brother. Naturally, I wanted to go along. He had met my son, my family, most of my friends and colleagues. (I was back working at the radio station, now not minding the commute because I could stay with him after my shows.) I had met two of his workmates and no one else. Literally no one else. I was more than ready to experience at least some of his life on his terms. My darling beau, on the other hand, seemed decidedly reluctant to book me a ticket.

"You'll be really bored," he said.

"My dad's house is small," he said.

"We mostly just hang out together, I do some work, we visit my brother, it's all very low key," he said.

I didn't care. I wanted to go. Back and forth the discussion went until finally I gave up. And gave in. But not before asking him point blank if he loved me. I had said it to him, not in an overly mushy, melodramatic way. More as a statement of fact like "I don't mind ironing your shirts because I love you." But he had yet to return the favour. He froze, but only momentarily, and then replied with those three beautiful words that every woman longs to hear:

"I don't know."

Yesiree, after seven months of dating, Robert did not know. But then he added with a smile, "But I also don't know that I don't love you."

Great. My scientist had suddenly become a politician.

I was exhausted from the battle and frustrated by the endless indecision. And so I suggested we enjoy the lead-up festive season, he jet off to England and I spend time with family and friends and then we "see where we're at" in January. I think this shocked him a bit and maybe even scared him. Especially when I said, "We will have plenty of time apart to think about things and decide how best to move forward." Almost three weeks to be exact. He was going for that long. I also then made the executive decision to take Jack to Mexico for a week right after New Year's. If I was going to be doing heavy thinking I wanted to do it under a palm tree with a cerveza in my hand.

December came and we partied, we visited, we shopped, we shared gifts and it was all fine and dandy and merry enough. And then the fateful day arrived. The morning that he flew, Robert said to me with complete sincerity, "Vickie, this break is going to be really good for us. Trust me. I really believe it is for the best."

Guess what? He was right. It was horrible while ongoing and I missed him immensely — even in Mexico with that blazing sun and palm trees galore. But that was also a good thing because it reminded me how invested I was. Turns out he felt the same. And when he returned to Canada our relationship bumped up a notch. For the first time I truly felt that he was all-in.

Did he tell me that he loved me? Well…no. At least not until our one-year anniversary, four months later, and in the midst of a fight no less. He had been invited to travel to New Zealand to deliver a paper and do some job reconnaissance. This was a good thing because he knew his tenure in Hamilton was ending that fall. I wasn't exactly desperate to move down under but I was willing to explore with him. Again he said "no." It would just be in and out. A quick ten days. All work. There was no point in me coming because he would be busy. Not worth the expense to me.

"Hey, it's my money," I countered. "And I'd like to go."

He was resolute. No. No. No.

And that was when I sort of lost it (who me?). I glared at him icily and snorted, "If you were me and you had just spent a year with someone who didn't want you to go home with him at Christmas and didn't want you to travel to New Zealand with him to possibly plan a future and couldn't even fucking say 'I love you' after a whole fucking year, well would you stay with that person?"

He was silent.

"Do you even love me?" I bellowed. Literally. I screamed it at his face.

His cheeks turned red and his eyes bulged and at the top of his lungs he bellowed back, "Yes, I love you Vickie!"

And there you have it. Romance at its finest. Two people in a kitchen screaming at each other, hostility stinking up the joint and passions running amok and finally my darling Robert and I were in love! Officially.

I was quite delighted. Still am. Robert and I are now in our eighth year of partnership and it's not always easy, but we keep working on being content and happy. After living with me in Meaford for six months (when his Hamilton gig ended) he ended up with a job at his dream university. Go on, guess where?

Guelph.

Yep, we moved back to Guelph. I was okay with the move because I still had lots of friends there (Shayann needed her mushrooms!) and it put me much closer to my aged mother and my son (pursuing a music career in Toronto).

Our five years back in Guelph were filled with love, laughter, arguments, struggles, wonder, magic, friendship and fruitful work. Just real life. And there was lots of activity in the kitchen. Shayann showing up for wine and mushrooms, Francis driving from Toronto frequently for fellowship and food, new friend and neighbour, Georgia, popping in and out like family, and lots of cooking and dinner parties.

Yes, the kitchen was still my happy place. So what did I learn to make for Robert? Well, he is a Brit after all and don't all Brits love a nice savory pot pie? This one can be created with virtually any filling you like. I've done beef and mushrooms, chicken and veg, even seafood in cream. Now, of course it's pretty easy to buy and heat a ready-made pot pie and some of them aren't bad. But where's the fun in that? And once you realize that frozen pie shells taste pretty damn good, it all becomes easy-peasy.

Pot Pies

Beef & Mushroom Filling

1 lb. ground beef or beef cubes, cut into bite-size morsels
mushrooms, sliced and sautéed
1 large onion, diced
2 carrots, chopped
3 celery stalks, chopped
1 can cream of mushroom soup
splash of white wine
fresh ground pepper, parsley, cloves — whatever seasonings you like!
2 frozen store-bought pie shells

Brown up the beef and onion, add the mushrooms (which you have already sautéed, clever chef that you are), carrots, celery and spices. If you want even more veg, go for it! Peas, corn, peppers, broccoli — whatever you like. Heat up the mushroom soup and wine in your microwave until smooth and creamy. For extra creamy, it turns out that adding cream helps.

Take your two frozen store-bought pie shells out of the freezer to thaw for five minutes, then prick them with a fork. Dump the beef/veg mixture into one, top with the other, pressing the sides down all around lest the yummy insides try to escape. Finally, lightly beat an egg (in a cup with a fork will do just fine) and brush the eggy glop onto the top crust. This will render it a lovely golden brown.

Bake at 400F for 45 minutes to an hour (on a cookie sheet to avoid trashing your oven just in case those insides do escape), add a pint of lager and you'll think you're at a pub over 'ome!

For chicken pie, simply substitute chicken morsels for the beef. I know. Smart, eh?

For seafood pie, I like to use shrimp, salmon chunks and any old fish (cod, halibut, tilapia) all sautéed together in lemon oil and kicky seafood spice. If you're in a super cheater mood you could also use canned tuna, salmon, clams, crab-meat — whatever your fishy heart desires!

PS: on the mushroom soup — any creamy canned soup will do the trick, so feel free to experiment. Chowder in the seafood pie? Cream of chicken in the chicken pie (what a surprise, I know), cream of celery, creamy cheese, cream of broccoli — why not? You can even use canned gravy or broth mixed with heavy cream.

I'm happy to report that Robert loves all of these pies and he loves them just as much the next day in his lunch!

Bucatini with Pecorino and Black Pepper

Before coming to Canada, but after earning two degrees in Scotland, Robert lived for three years in Italy on the shores of Laggo Maggiori (right next door to Lake Como). Oh how I wish I had known him then, loving all things Italian as I do. The language. The loafers. The food! He often raved about the simplicity of Italian cooking, especially when it comes to pasta. I discovered this dish at a restaurant in Toronto and it was most definitely love at first bite. I was dining with Jack and his girlfriend and even though they had both ordered pizza, once they tasted the bucatini they ordered it for dessert, that's how damn delicious it is.

Bucatini I had never even heard of this type of pasta before and it's not always easy to find, but it has become my new go-to (even for Bolognaise sauce) so when I find it, I really stock up. It is much like spaghetti, just fatter and round (unlike linguine).

Pecorino Romano cheese usually found at your more upscale (or Italian) supermarkets. Hard like Parmesan but saltier.

fresh ground pepper

fresh basil, torn

splash of garlic olive oil or big blob of butter

fresh aruqula

Grate a healthy portion of pecorino. When I say healthy I mean lots, like maybe a full cup if you're making dinner for two.

Boil the bucatini in water as directed. When it is ready (al dente) strain the water, holding some back (I strain directly into an oversized measuring cup).

Sauté the pasta in oil or butter, adding the cheese in small increments. Now you must keep stirring, stirring, stirring and then add the pasta water also in small increments. This is what stops the cheese from globbing. Just make sure you stir hard! Top with loads of fresh ground pepper and fresh torn basil. Serve on a bed of fresh arugula (no dressing) and you will have one of the most simple, elegant, yummy dinner party meals of all time. Quite often when I serve this for friends, I start the meal with a creamy, spicy seafood chowder (see below).

Tomato/Bacon Bucatini

And another variation — this is Fran's absolute favourite.

Pecorino Romano cheese, or asiago or Parmesan *(any hard Italian cheese)*

whole bunch of grape tomatoes, chopped

1 box precooked bacon, chopped

fresh ground pepper

fresh rosemary (ripped from the stalk) **or dried** (whole bunch)

splash of garlic olive oil

fresh arugula

Boil the bucatini and drain. Sauté the tomatoes and bacon in garlic olive oil, then add the rosemary and pepper. Add the cheese and the cooked bucatini. Mix it all together and serve over fresh arugula.

Kicky Seafood Chowder

---

1 package frozen fish (you choose — salmon, cod, halibut, sole... just not the battered kind), thawed

1 package frozen shrimp (uncooked), thawed

2 cartons vegetable broth

2 fish bouillon cubes

1/2 cup fresh tomatoes, diced (you could also use canned)

1/2 cup corn (frozen or canned)

1/2 litre heavy cream (35%)

1 Tbsp. kicky seafood seasoning (you buy this pre-mixed at the supermarket. President's Choice has a great one)

fresh ground pepper

large splash of lemon olive oil

chives and parsley (fresh or dried)

Sauté the fish and shrimp in the lemon oil. Most times I don't even bother cutting up the fish in advance. I find that most thawed frozen fish will just break apart with the spoon as you are frying. Add the kicky seafood seasoning while you stir. When the fish looks cooked (not gelatinous), cover (just barely) with water and boil hard. Boil until the liquid is reduced but not dry. Add the broth, tomatoes, corn and bouillon cubes and simmer for about 15 minutes. Then add the cream (which you may want to heat up in the microwave first to prevent curdling) and parsley. Taste the soup and if it's good, leave it. If not add some pepper for more zing. Serve topped with chives.

And then for dessert...

Dark Chocolate Coconut Blobs

As mentioned before, I'm not much of a baker and I don't worry a lot about creating fancy desserts. I love ice cream, sorbet, frozen yogurt, brownies and the occasional profiterole, pie or slice of decadent birthday cake. But I do absolutely love really good dark chocolate and coconut. Thus was born this simple little treat that Georgia has lovingly labeled "the only dessert you will ever need to eat, ever again."

---

1 package quality dark chocolate I buy mine in the baking aisle but even a couple of large bars of your fave will work

2/3 package unsweetened coconut

1/4 cup oatmeal

1/4 cup heavy cream (35%)

splash of Grand Marnier

Optional: Skor bits

In the top of a double boiler, melt the chocolate, stirring constantly. Add the cream (more stirring). After removing the pot from the heat, add the coconut and oatmeal. Here is where you'll need to experiment to find your desired consistency. Just remember these will be turning into blobs so don't use too much liquid. And if you're drinking wine and find that you have used too much liquid (oops!) just add more coconut. Or oatmeal. At the end, toss in that splash of Grande Marnier. If you're a non-drinker don't worry, it's not essential. Just yummy.

Lay out sheets of parchment paper and, using two teaspoons, drop your beauteous blobs onto it. Make them as big or as small as you like. After an hour or so of cooling on the counter, refrigerate. I keep mine in the fridge until they are gone. Then Georgia comes over and we make more.

Robert is a big fan of the "bitchin' kitchen" even when he is the only man present. He knows that sooner or later something yummy will be served and he is quite happy to contribute his manly two cents to whatever conversational topic is on tap. And my girlfriends all adore him. So does my son and my family.

As it turns out, so do I.

We have now relocated back to Meaford. Robert's tenure at the University of Guelph ended and we decided semi-retirement was in order. I still do my radio work and he is working with his hands, something he said he "fancied doing" after all those years of brain industry. We have a little summer place up on The Bruce Peninsula (my favourite place in the world) and we enjoy every moment there. Who knows? Maybe we'll move there full-time one day. It's all about the adventure. Taking each day as it comes and making every moment count. We don't always succeed but we are always aware. This is not an effortless pursuit. I have learned that anything worthwhile takes work. Our love has matured, deepened and maybe even mellowed. Not without challenges and conflict. But with conviction. We are in this for the long haul and have committed to each other and our future.

Is this my Disney ending? Well, no. Probably because I am no longer a Disney girl. This is just where I am at right now, today. School of hard knocks attended, lessons learned, regrets acknowledged and wisdom gained. Today. It is a good place. A contented place. A place I never expected to want and a place I often believed I didn't deserve. But it is my place. And Robert's place. And Shiloh's place. Jack's place too when he can join us.

I will never again attempt to guess the future. Or even plan too much of the future. Remember when I said, "Never say never and never say forever"? There are people who will say, "Easy way out, Vickie. Grow up and make a commitment and honour it!" Well, okay then. I commit to being honest. I commit to working on all my relationships. I commit to open communication and regular, soul-baring dialogue when required. I commit to making the effort, telling the truth and doing the work.

And one last thing: I commit to *only* cheating in the kitchen. And that's a promise.

Epilogue

LIFE GOES ON, THIS WE ALL KNOW. Life goes on and I am grateful for every single day. I look back on these last sixteen years with fondness, sadness, a bit of incredulity and maybe a tiny bit of regret. I do try to keep regret to a minimum though, and for a very good reason. I live a fully authentic life now. A life in its own moment. A life not guided by fairy tales or Disney dreams, Pepsi commercials or doing what I'm supposed to do. A lovely life rooted in a reality I have fashioned and worked on. Worked on hard.

I love that this has been MY work. I think HBS was right when he said I had to leave him not for Grover but for ME. I had to grow up, woman up and rescue my own ass. Lean on my friends and lean on myself. Learn to appreciate the journey, warts and all, and learn to live in truth. That is the big one.

I've pretty much lost contact with my yoga-prince, Charlie. We are friends on Facebook, have shared an occasional email or phone call and even had drinks and dinner several years ago (the Bruce #3 era) when Cassandra and I ventured to Vancouver to visit her daughter who was attending university there. From what I could tell, Charlie was the same. Filled with life wisdom, which he is always eager to share. He is dynamic, engaging and still darn fine looking. I look back on my dalliance with Charlie as such a vital stepping-stone in my personal evolution because he compelled me to look at life, love and relationships in a whole new light. One which continues to shine, sometimes brightly, often just a flicker, but always plugged in. He inspired me to:

Try to keep that "Disney Girl" at bay.

Live in the moment as it is, not as I envisioned it or hoped it would be.

Expectations = Disappointment.

Try to keep that "Disney Girl" at bay.

When I think of Charlie now, I always smile. Is there a "what if?" No, not even a tiny one. Mostly I just feel gratitude that he was such a vital bridge between my old Grover life and my future "more evolved" life. If you look back at those old emails you'll see I truly thought Grover was my Prince Charming. And I truly thought that once I found him, I would finally be happy. I mean, after all the sadness, I would finally experience life as it should be, filled with honest, undeniable, passionate, all-consuming love. The love I had waited for my whole life.

Not so much. As we've all learned, it's what comes after "The End" that makes the relationship interesting. Even though Grover and I found love, we couldn't *live* love. Charlie allowed me to understand that that's okay. It's not about the ending. It's about the learning and it's about being open to the journey. And I still do yoga!

As for Ben, we are still in touch. Very sporadically but we still completely adore and care about one another. He said, "friends for life" and life ain't over yet. I'm ever-hopeful that our friendship will continue, one day I'll bake another gluten free chocolate pie for him, we'll sing a few songs and share a few laughs. Ben will always be special to me.

Then there's Billy. Ah Billy. Such a sweetheart and such a goof. He once said to me (shortly before we broke up), "I'm starting to believe I can't actually be with anybody — and I'm okay with that." I'm starting to believe he is right. We did see each other in Southampton a few times post-breakup. The first was a couple of months after the split, when Fran and I rented a place on the water for a few nights and decided to knock on his door spur of the moment. The three of us shared wine and cocktail conversation and just before we left, Billy offered up what was probably the biggest, strongest hug of our entire acquaintance. Later that evening, after a gray and gloomy day, more wine and a few too many tipsy tears, the clouds parted for a moment and he texted me: *Looks like we might get a sunset after all.*

That was it. Knowing Billy as I did, it was pretty profound. He was reaching out in the best way he could. Not to reconnect as lovers but to at least try to end it with love. I have no idea where he is now or what he is doing. I'm okay with that. That chapter is completely closed. Closed with gratitude. Because Billy was yet another stepping-stone on my path and, like all the others, propelled me forward to my next life lesson.

Onwards to Bruce #2. Surprisingly enough, in spite of the fact that our break-up wasn't exactly bloodless, we remained in touch via email for several years. I find that the more content I become, the less energy I am willing to expend on tortured souls. I would never write one off completely just because they are difficult. I know that beneath all that torture, there is a fragile soul desperate for love. Been there, done that, am that. So Bruce #2 will always have a place in my heart and, if he wants it, in my life. Like I said, just because romantic love isn't a possibility doesn't mean that love doesn't still exist. It should. And it does. Friendship love is a damn fine thing.

Then there is Bruce #3. We're friends on Facebook and he came to Jack's CD release party last summer. He has a new partner and seems to be doing well. This makes me very happy. Bruce has a huge heart and an honest soul. We had a good run, made some awesome memories and we tried our damndest. We just didn't have the ability to compromise as much as was needed to go the distance. But no regrets! Bruce will always own a corner of my heart.

And what about those exes? You know, my ex-husband and Grover's ex-wife. After sixteen years together it looks like they are still going strong, faithfully united and pretty darn happy about it. How do I know? Well, when Jack turned eighteen I asked him how he wanted to celebrate his birthday. He replied that he wanted dinner out with Bruce and me, plus Dad and his gal. All together. In the same city. Same restaurant. Same table!

"Ha!" thought I. *Snowball's chance in hell.* But I put forth the suggestion to HBS, knowing that there would be some serious *'splaining to do* if they took a pass. This was Jack's test and he was just waiting for someone to fail. That someone being Kay. Seven years had passed and she still wasn't giving an inch. To me.

Surprisingly, they showed up. Not for dinner, mind you, but for dessert. The five of us sat in a large booth, conversed civilly, feted our child and made it through the hour without daggers or insults. As we returned to the car Jack said, "Well, that went well, didn't it?"

Indeed it had. And it was just the beginning.

Six months later I hosted a high school graduation party for Jack — in my Guelph home — and once again they came. They ate my food, drank my wine, conversed with my guests and actually seemed to have a good time. Holy cow!

Summer came and went and every time our paths crossed the ice melted just a little bit more. By the time Christmas rolled around and Jack returned to Canada for his school break, the happy couple was not only willing to drive to Meaford to pick him up, but they were willing to stay for lunch! After which they invited us to pop in for a drink on Christmas Day when we would be fetching Jack. It was all terribly convivial and I will tell you there were even hugs involved. Hugs with everyone!

The day before Jack flew back to California, we all met up at a restaurant once again to celebrate his nineteenth birthday. I was feeling a bit under the weather and disinclined to hug anyone, lest I spread the love. But Kay walked right up to me and demanded her sugar. Kay wanted a hug!

Well knock me down with a feather! How could I say no?

All I can say now is I AM THRILLED! This is a much better life for me and a much better life for Jack. Maybe there was no official "forgiveness" but that's okay. What's important is that we are all moving forward — with love. With love and kindness and the acceptance that this is our new reality, now let's make the best of it.

Kinda wacky, eh?

Since Robert and I have been together we have socialized with HBS and Kay several times. We all hung out at Jack's big party last year. Her brother had just died and I was really surprised and grateful that in spite of her pain she had come to support Jack. At the end of his show she came right up to me (in the middle of the dance floor where I was the adoring mother in the crowd), patted me on the back and offered *me* congratulations. Needless to say I was a tad surprised.

"Thank you, he was great wasn't he?" I was beaming.

"Yes he was. He did amazing. You should be so proud!"

"I am! I am bursting! And you should be proud too. Because we are all a team. We are Jack's team. He loves us all and we are all his team."

We hugged it out.

A few days later she called me. I was blown away when I saw her name on my screen.

"I just had to call you to congratulate you on your son. What a wonderful night that was for him!"

"Um, thanks but, um, Kay, you know you already did that. On Friday night?"

"I did?"

Laughing. "Yes you did. We had a big moment out on the dance floor, remember?"

She is laughing now too. "Oh my goodness, I have to tell you, what with my brother dying and dental surgery meaning I couldn't eat and then drinking too much free tequila and well...doesn't matter. He just did such a great show and I wanted to tell you."

We were on the phone for almost an hour. And it was good. We hashed out a few old woes, talked about our kids and at one point she admitted, "HBS has been a godsend." This is the truth. HBS was her godsend. IS her godsend. During one of our early accidental phone calls, when she and HBS had been together for almost a year, she chastised me harshly for abandoning this man who had loved me so strongly and treated me so well. I suggested quietly that perhaps the HBS she knew was just a bit different than the HBS to whom I had been married. Perhaps SHE had brought out a different side of him? Perhaps he had learned a few things and was now putting these lessons into practice? Indeed, even Jack once confessed to me that his father was a new man. More loving, more attentive, more present in the relationship. Jack's theory was that his father had learned his lesson the hard way and wasn't about to make the same mistake again.

Does that make me bitter? This is the part where I'm pretty sure you expect me to assert *Not one bit! I'm all lovey-dovey altruistically ecstatic for them!*

Well, I am happy for them. I am happy they found each other and have made a happy life. Do I wish HBS had learned these lessons during our marriage? Of course. Do I wish I had learned a whole lot of lessons during our marriage? Of course. We didn't. And now our new partners are reaping the benefits of our old mistakes and our hard-won education.

The thing is, in hindsight I believe HBS and I could have had a good marriage. With honest dialogue and therapy and loads of hard work we could have forged a viable union. He is an amazingly unique individual and I'm quite (painfully) sure I took that for granted for far too many years. But when trains leave the station *they leave the station.* Sure the Grover train left (with me on board) but so did the HBS/Kay train. And once that one hit the tracks there was no turning back. For any of us.

HBS and I are okay. Not great, but okay. We don't share the loving friendship I wish we did. We only socialize when Jack's music is involved. We most likely don't really understand each other any better now than we did when we were married. It's funny how right after I left him he treated me with more love, kindness and presence than he does now, sixteen years later. I guess time does heal all wounds and his healing is best served by my absence.

Fair enough.

We can still be funny (kinda) though. Case in point: when we were together I always wanted a swimming pool and he never wanted to give me one (too much work). As soon as Kay moved in they got a pool. I mentioned the great unfairness of this one day when he came to pick up Jack and stayed for a beer.

"Maybe if you'd stayed longer you would have got the pool!" he said.

Ha ha.

I also always wanted him to dance with me, something he was perennially reluctant to do. He took dance lessons with Kay. At my niece's wedding they enthusiastically cut some jolly rugs whilst I (dateless) looked after my mother. When HBS came to bid my mom adieu I commented on his newfound interest in tripping the light fantastic. He just grinned sheepishly. And so I went for the kill: "Maybe if you had danced with me I would have stayed longer."

Bam.

I can only hope that as time marches on we will find something more than détente to colour our interactions. As I once told him (and believe with all my heart) we are family. Forever. We made a family and we are a family. It is up to us to define the new parameters, but we are still and always will be a family.

Which leads to Grover (since he and Kay are also family forever). He and I are no longer in touch. We had a brief text exchange (instigated by me) when his father died, nothing when my mother died (maybe no one told him?) and then one more last summer. As you know, I never say never and I never say forever. I do know finally, after all these years, that I must put Grover, our past and his current life (whatever that is) into a little box and store it at the back of my mental closet. I truly believed he was the love of my life. Obviously he was not. I have come to believe that some of us get many loves in our lives. And that is as far as I need to go to quantify it. Yes, I will always love him. For all the trauma and suffering and guilt and tears and turmoil, Grover's love was special. Grover was special. And I will always choose to love him.

There is a line in the song *I Can Let Go Now* written by Michael McDonald: *I was tossed high by love I almost never came down, only to land here where love's no longer found, where I'm no longer bound and I can let go now.*

I texted these words to Grover. Because that was me. Tossed high by love. But yes, I can let go now. No matter what anyone else chooses, I can let go with love.

Robert and I are still in it. And as much as I suspect you're looking for a textbook happy ending filled with resolution and hearts and balloons, I'm not going to give it to you. Because I truly am no longer a Disney Girl. This little "cook-moir" is a snapshot of sixteen years of my life. There was much life before and (I hope) much life still to come. I look to two of my favourite authors — Elizabeth Gilbert and Glennon Doyle — and to the conclusion of their memoirs. Both looking towards happily-ever-after with their men. Until in real life they both fall in love with other women. Everything changes and new books are written.

Life is funny that way. Just when you think you've got it all figured out that curve ball smacks you in the head. So I now choose to look at my life as a process. A journey. A progression. An evolution. I'm a much better cook than I was sixteen years ago and I'd like to think I'm a much better mate too. I'm certainly a much more honest mate. A much more informed mate. And a much more present mate. All of which (I hope) bodes well for my future with Robert. Actually, I trust it will bode well with all of my relationships.

Sure, I am still Vickie van Dyke, proud cheater. But only in the kitchen.

Acknowledgements

This book has been a long time in the making. Like twelve years long. I would write, file away, write some more, edit, file away, ignore for months and on and on it would go. I could never get it to *feel* right, and so I could never send it off into the universe with confidence. It feels right now. It feels honest and still (I hope) kind. I am so very grateful to every single chapter and every single character.

Big thanks to Jacqui Brown, my soul sister in scribbling and smooth jazz. You believed in this book from the get-go and here we finally are.

Colleen M (my first editor), Debbie G, Julie L, Caroline D, Angie R, Margaret B, Deborah H, Corina B and Marlene B and Ellen V — my early readers, commenters, armchair editors and friends. Your help was invaluable.

Bibi — thank you for your inspired artwork.

My late mother, Sarah Dyck, who always championed my writing even when she was unsure of its content. Or style. She inspired me to publish and I hope she would be proud.

Author Terry Fallis (read his books!) — thank you for paying it forward.

Elizabeth Gilbert — you taught me (unknowingly) that the only voice I needed to find was the one I already had. Thank you.

To all the fabulous friends who have dined chez moi, thank you for your smiles, your ears, your hugs and your taste buds. You got me through some pretty tough times and I am forever grateful.

To all the men I've loved before (that should be a song, right?), I will never forget you and in some back corner of my heart I will always cherish you. Thank you for the lessons and the love.

And to Richard — thank you for staying by my side through a million edits, out-loud reads, content discussions, confessions, revelations and truths. It takes a special kind of man to live through a book like this when the author is his love. That is you.

About the Author
Vickie van Dyke

Vickie has enjoyed a multitude of colourful and creative careers. With a BA in drama and a wealth of amateur and semi-professional stage experience under her belt, she landed her first paid gig in summer stock musical theatre before joining a touring pop group. Eventually she formed her own country rock band, writing and recording several original compositions. After a brief stint on the business side of music handling record promotions for an independent firm, she segued into country radio. Heard on 820 CHAM-Hamilton for ten years in the early morning and midday slots, she also pre-recorded a pop show for a sister station in London. She hosted her own television show (*Showdown*), wrote for television (*The Canadian Country Music Awards* on CTV), radio (numerous specials) and a bi-weekly newspaper column (*Country Corner*) for the *Hamilton Spectator*.

Vickie helmed the midday show at Canada's premier smooth jazz outlet, Wave 94.7FM from its launch in 2000 until 2011. She also penned the script for the annual Canadian Smooth Jazz Awards for all seven years and was named the first ever Canadian Smooth Jazz Broadcaster of the Year in 2007. She is currently the morning host at www.wave.fm and occasionally performs pop jazz and jazz standards. Other recent written works include a cabaret-style musical *My Romance* (workshop production available on YouTube) featuring the classics of Rodgers and Hart. Her blog can be found at **WineSoakedRamblings.com** (*because the drunken pen writes the sober heart*).

Currently living on Georgian Bay with Shiloh and Richard, Vickie continues to scribble, make music, support her son Sam Drysdale's musical career whole-heartedly and cook for all her friends. Watch for an upcoming YouTube channel — The Potty-Mouthed Chef!

Facebook vickie.van.dyke
Twitter @vickievandyke
Instagram @vickievandyke
Blog winesoakedramblings.com
Email pottymouthedchef@gmail.com
Website pottymouthedchef.ca

CPSIA information can be obtained
at www.ICGtesting.com
Printed in the USA
LVHW020019270620
659094LV00002B/223